THE FOUR
& TWENTY
BLACKBIRDS
PIE BOOK

THE FOUR & TWENTY BLACKBIRDS PIE BOOK

UNCOMMON RECIPES FROM THE CELEBRATED BROOKLYN PIE SHOP

EMILY ELSEN & MELISSA ELSEN

Photography by Gentl & Hyers

GRAND CENTRAL
Life & Style
NEW YORK · BOSTON

Grand Central Life & Style
Hachette Book Group
237 Park Avenue
New York, NY 10017

www.GrandCentralLifeandStyle.com

Printed in the United States of America

Q-MA

First Edition: October 2013
10 9 8 7 6 5 4 3 2 1

Grand Central Life & Style is an imprint of Grand Central Publishing.
The Grand Central Life & Style name and logo are trademarks of
Hachette Book Group, Inc.

The Hachette Speakers Bureau provides a wide range of authors for
speaking events. To find out more, go to www.HachetteSpeakersBureau
.com or call (866) 376-6591.

The publisher is not responsible for websites (or their content) that are
not owned by the publisher.

Library of Congress Control Number: 2013939669

For our mom & dad

In loving memory of our grandparents:

Elizabeth and Frank, Frances and Marvin

Contents

Spring

Fall

Winter

Crusts

THE FOUR
& TWENTY
BLACKBIRDS
PIE BOOK

An Introduction

Sisters

As siblings, we are very close in age, which makes us practically peers. Growing up in a small midwestern town where we graduated high school with the same fifteen kids we went to elementary school with, we managed to keep a firm sense of independence and to pursue our own interests and friendships (thanks in a large part to a strong mother intent on raising us and our brother, Chris, as self-determined people). Though we shared a bedroom, teachers, basketball coaches, and after-school activities during our school years, we followed very different paths after high school—Emily to New York City and London for art school, and Melissa, after finishing a degree in finance, on an extended work visa journey through Australia and New Zealand—before reconnecting to live together again in an old house in Crown Heights, Brooklyn, where we would eventually discover a mutual love for pie baking and turn it into our livelihood.

Family Business

The Calico Kitchen, on Main Street in Hecla, South Dakota (population 230), was our second home as kids; our playground for creativity; our venue for weekend breakfasts, high school lunch breaks, and after-school hangouts; the site of our first job (dishwasher), second job (waitress), and third job (cook); and the backbone of our family life. Founded, owned, and operated by our mother and her sisters, Susan and Anne, the restaurant absolutely defined a community gathering place—serving lunch to the region's farmers, banquets to the local bowling team, meals to the wild game hunters who traveled from afar for the abundant local pheasant- and deer-hunting seasons, coffee to the after-church crowd, and annual prom banquets to the high school students.

Over the years we held family gatherings there—especially when all our aunts, uncles, and cousins made it back to town for a holiday—and the restaurant would be filled to capacity with just family. Mother's Day was one of the biggest days of the year at the Calico and was always a special time to be working together in the kitchen with Mom and our aunts, serving breakfast, lunch, and dinner to our close-knit community of mothers and their families. Every day, it was the norm to be surrounded by hardworking

women in white aprons simultaneously handling the grill, the oven, or the fryer; washing the dishes; prepping the potatoes; carving the meat; and, yes, baking the pies. And there was one special woman who baked all those ever-popular pies, our grandmother Liz.

Elizabeth Zastrow was born and raised in our little town of Hecla in the house her parents built. After helping raise her brothers and sisters, she moved to Chicago to work as a nanny, but eventually returned home to care for her mother. She met our grandfather Frank when he came to town with his passel of hunting dogs looking for a place to board; he rented a room in the ample upstairs, which Grandma and her mother maintained as a sort of local inn. Grandma Liz always joked that at thirty years old she was an old maid and never expected to marry. But Frank took a liking to Liz and won her heart and hand in marriage, and within ten years they had seven children, who were also raised in that very same house.

We love to tell the story that our parents, Mary and Ron, met while working for Frohling's Jack & Jill, the local butcher, and it's true; our dad broke down animals and cut the meat, and our mom worked the counter, weighing and wrapping it to order for customers. It should come as little surprise that they would both venture in their early twenties into food-related businesses in their hometown—our mother with her restaurant and our father with his own grain-farming operation, which he started with the help of his mother, Frances, and father, Marvin—both with a true passion and dedication to making their enterprises succeed. It was our father who instilled in us that working for yourself is the only way to go; "make your own raises," he would advise.

The first recipes for Four & Twenty Blackbirds were devised in the kitchen of a turn-of-the-century mansion in Crown Heights, Brooklyn—aka our apartment. After our college years and a few post-college years working, we found ourselves living together again as sisters, sharing a bathroom, a kitchen, and eventually a sky-blue 1990 Toyota Camry wagon.

Having an ample kitchen space in our home to entertain and cook for friends certainly had some influence in fostering our idea of starting a pie company—whenever we planned a dinner party, we tested a new pie or tart recipe. For what is making a recipe without sharing it? The sincere and enduring encouragement of some of our dearest friends was fuel for our fire. It helped us believe in ourselves; it gave us confidence that as self-taught bakers we could make a go of it without a culinary degree or formal training, or a startup budget to speak of.

Why Pie?

The earliest days of our business planning happened at a time when the economy was in a major downturn: Melissa, having graduated with a degree in finance, was able to find only part-time work as a waitress in Brooklyn, while Emily maintained a full-time day job in photography. We would spend any and all spare time planning recipes and trading ideas, deliberating over what to name our company, how to brand it, what sort of identity we wanted it to have, and most important, how to make and sell the most delicious pie in New York City. At the time, we were hard-pressed to find anyone focusing exclusively on pies in a truly handmade way, using seasonal and fresh ingredients sourced from local orchards. Sure, plenty of bakeries made and carried pies, but not pies like ours; and we didn't know of any places in the neighborhoods we frequented that were dedicated exclusively to the experience of sitting down and eating a slice of pie with a cup of coffee. Perhaps such a place existed, but not on our radar, and that is exactly what we wanted to create: a local pie shop.

In the early days of our pie making and baking together, we would take on any variety of baking opportunities that came our way—from food-styling jobs (Christmas cookies in July for QVC or *Star Wars*–themed birthday cakes for Target) to wedding catering and private parties (Melissa single-handedly made and baked hundreds of gougères in the summer heat in our home oven for a wedding party)—and we have many friends to thank for connecting us with customers and being supportive of our ambitions. Some of our most exciting and challenging projects were for our friends Miranda Lloyd and Eugene Jho, who hosted impressive multicourse dinner parties in their loft in Bushwick. They would devise a highly creative menu of course upon course, along with cocktails and wines, and then ask us to create a pie or tart dessert that worked with the meal. It was inspiring in the most wonderful way and laid the groundwork for us to build confidence in serving our product to complete strangers. We would prepare the dessert at home, drive it over to their place midparty, sneak in, plate, and serve. We quickly came to realize that one of the most valuable parts of this experience was getting to talk with the guests about what they liked and didn't like in our recipes.

Throughout this time, we knew our pies were our strongest suit, and that which inspired us most. By the time Thanksgiving of 2009 rolled around, we found ourselves with a slew of pie orders to make just for friends and family, with the promise that they would be hand-delivered straight from our home kitchen.

Spotting a storefront for rent on the corner of Third Avenue and Eighth Street is what really spurred the leap from home kitchen to our own brick-and-mortar space. Our ambitions and expectations for our pie shop were very simple: to create a gathering place to support and serve our community with really good pie and coffee—both of us knowing well from our upbringing and the way we like to eat that quality and execution of product are far more important than being trendy or cashing in on a passing fad, and that substance over simply sugar is what keeps customers coming back.

The Four & Twenty Blackbirds Pie Shop

We signed the lease for our pie shop location on New Year's Eve with a blue moon in the sky overhead. With the help of friends, we started demolition the very next day, January 1, 2010, tearing down layers of dirty old plaster, outdated ceiling board, and old plastic flooring to reveal the true character of our space: original tin walls and hardwood flooring, a classic Brooklyn look. We had to design and rebuild the entire place to be perfect for pie baking and pie eating. Our talented, carpentry-savvy friends Inez Valk-Kempthorne and Justus Kempthorne helped us every step of the way. We wanted ample seating and a visible open kitchen for our customers to see what's going on in the back. After three months of hard work, we opened our doors to the public in April of 2010, and that's when we really began to understand what the pie business was all about.

To say our kitchen space is small would be an understatement. It is, however, efficient, and our one convection oven works as hard as we do. In the early days, we would bake until late in the night, oftentimes well past one in the morning, only to be back in at five a.m. to bake the morning pastry—including our Egg in a Nest and Blackbird's Bread—and open our doors for our eager neighborhood customers. We very naively thought we could do everything ourselves at least for the first couple of weeks, but quickly realized that was entirely impossible and we needed to hire some help. Now, years later, we have a small but highly talented group of pie and pastry makers who take what they do very seriously and care deeply about making the best products possible. Our kitchen team, baristas, and dishwashers, are the backbone of the experience our customers have at the shop, and we couldn't run our place without each and every one of them.

Opposite: Our friend and pie shop neighbor Oona Brennan has been a pie shop apprentice since we opened our doors; her favorite pie is strawberry balsamic.

How to Use This Book

The decision to organize the recipes in this book seasonally was obvious: in the pie shop we bake pies according to the season and the ingredients available, and all our recipes revolve around that approach. Simple, logical—and that's how our grandma did it too.

The idea of a seasonal pie shop was actually somewhat unusual to more than a handful of our customers in the early days—not to mention that we decided to unearth and update all kinds of old-fashioned recipes with weird names like "chess" and "black bottom" and use ingredients uncommon to New Yorkers, such as gooseberries and wild ginger. Some customers expected us to offer every kind of pie under the sun and to serve peach pies in December. We've taken it as an opportunity to share the knowledge that fruit (and all food, for that matter) in season and freshly picked tastes best and, by virtue of that, makes sense. Trends aside, this is how we grew up eating—with a bountiful garden in the summertime, and much of that bounty either frozen or home-canned for eating in the wintertime.

Fruit that is picked before it's ripe, boxed, and shipped thousands of miles will never taste as good as fruit that's grown nearby and picked at full ripeness. Make it your motto to bake pies when fruit is in season and to use the fruit that grows in your region. We know that it is sometimes impossible to get certain fruits in certain areas, so if you can't get your hands on the fruit you really want to bake with locally, try experimenting with fruits you can get—substituting those that are similar in structure and water content. We do source some fruits such as citrus and figs from the West Coast, as it has an abundance of quality produce and it isn't too far away—but, again, we purchase only what is in season there.

For each recipe we've suggested a crust pairing, and we tell you on which page the recipe for that crust appears. As a general rule, you will want to prepare your crust before starting on the filling. Many of our crust recipes (such as the All-Butter, the Lard & Butter, and the Chocolate All-Butter) can be made a week or more in advance and wrapped and frozen until you need them. Just thaw at room temperature or overnight in the refrigerator.

We encourage you to try different crusts with different pies; be experimental, and don't be afraid to make your own adjustments and modifications. Add or take away, be inspired and let your creativity loose, for pie is nothing if not an endless playground for interpretation.

Make a point to read through the recipe you are about to make in its entirety before jumping in. Read the "Techniques" section (see page 48) of this book before you begin the recipes as well—it will answer many questions that you may have and give you guidance on how to execute certain steps, such as rolling out your dough and fitting it into the pie pan. Reference this section as needed while you work through the recipes.

If you do any sort of baking or cooking already, you know the importance of "mise en place" or "everything in its place." That's the technique professionals use, and there is a reason. Set yourself and your workspace up with the tools and ingredients you need to complete your recipe (you won't want to be searching for a sieve while your pistachio coconut cream filling is about to curdle on the stove top). Creating a good atmosphere should be your priority as well; it is a very important part of our workday—music, good lighting, and a clean and organized workspace are major factors in creating good pies. Set up such a space for yourself before you begin and your pie will come out better—we promise.

We've given you our tips and tricks based on what we've learned from making pie every day for a good while now, but that is not to say we haven't missed some good ideas or you won't disagree with us. Don't be afraid to modify and make the pies your own. Why else would we share our recipes with you? We honed our skills as pie makers by reading and listening to what other people did before us and then tweaking ingredients and techniques to our liking. In fact, if you've got ideas or suggestions you'd like to share with us, we'd love to hear from you. One of the best things about making pie is sharing your approach with other pie makers. True pie makers love to talk about pie.

Following the Recipes

Making a pie from start to finish takes time, no matter what your skill level. All in one go, you'll need to allot at least 3 to 4 hours from crust making to eating for a fruit pie, and even more for a custard pie, which usually requires prebaking of the crust.

Slicing into a warm fruit pie is one of the high points of pie baking, but if you slice too soon after baking, the juices won't have thickened and the pie will be soup; the same is true for custards. You'll want to plan accordingly so that your hard work isn't for naught.

The following is a general outline for making the pies in this book. Read the individual recipe thoroughly for extra steps or variations as well as advance preparation tips, and make sure you have read the "Techniques" section regarding the type of crust you will be preparing.

Prepare the pie dough: You need to prepare dough at least 30 minutes (preferably 1 to 2 hours) and up to 3 days before rolling, so that the dough has time to rest and the glutens are allowed to relax, and so that you can chill it thoroughly before working with it. Unbaked dough wrapped in plastic can also be frozen for up to 1 month.

Roll out the dough: Roll out the dough as required by the recipe (see page 54 for directions). After rolling, the dough will need to chill again for at least 30 minutes to relax the glutens, especially if the shell is going to be prebaked.

Prepare the filling: This step can come before or after rolling. For fruit pies, consider the prep involved (coring and peeling, for example) and whether or not the fruit needs to macerate first. Custards are relatively straightforward, though it's best, and sometimes required (as for cream cheese), for ingredients to be at room temperature when mixing. Most custards can be made up to 3 days ahead of time and refrigerated until needed, though they should be removed from the fridge to take off some of the chill 15 to 20 minutes before using; then they should be stirred well.

Prebake, if necessary: Some recipes require a prebaked crust. See pages 68–69 for detailed instructions.

Assembly: For fruit pies, transfer the filling to the shell, leaving behind excess juice, arrange the lattice or place the top crust, and crimp as desired (see pages 58 and 64 for lattice and crimping directions). For best results, chill the whole pie for 10 to 15 minutes before applying the egg wash and baking. Most custard pies are simply poured into the shell and baked. However, check the recipe for detailed instructions.

Baking: Baking times can range from 30 to 55 minutes for a custard pie more than 1 hour for a fruit pie. **A note about temperatures:** all temperatures given in this book are for baking in a glass pie pan unless otherwise noted. If using a metal pan, lower the temperature by 25°F, as metal conducts heat more quickly but less evenly than glass.

Cooling: Fruit pies should cool for a minimum of 1 to 2 hours. Custard pies must cool to room temperature, or very near, up to 2 hours.

Our grandma Liz's recipe box.

Ingredients

Butter

The most important ingredient in making a delicious piecrust is good, fresh butter. We use unsalted, high-fat butter—82% or more fat content—often called European-style. Plugra is a good, readily available option, as is Cabot. If you can't get your hands on either of these, you can definitely use a standard butter, but it should be sweet (unsalted) butter for sure.

Flour

For a readily available flour, we recommend Hecker's all-purpose unbleached flour. Gold Medal is also good. No matter the brand, make sure to use unbleached flour. We find that using pastry flour results in a subpar, sandier, less flaky crust. Organic flour is increasingly available on the market; if you can find it, all the better.

Eggs

For the recipes in this book, you will want to use large eggs. Finding locally grown, farm-fresh eggs shouldn't be that difficult, so make an effort to get some—the flavor and richness of fresh eggs are so much better than those of commercially produced eggs. At the very least, make an effort to get cage-free eggs.

Cream and Milk

Using a fresh, high-quality heavy cream (preferably not the ultra-pasteurized kind) is an absolute must; it is pricey but totally worth it. We use a cream with 40% milk fat content, though you can substitute cream with a lower milk fat content if that's what is available to you. Battenkill Valley Creamery is our favorite source for milk; it is small and local. Get your fresh dairy as close to home as possible.

Fruit

In the previous section, you will have noticed our emphasis on fresh, local, and seasonal when it comes to fruit. Try your hardest to get your fruits locally. If you don't have enough of one kind of fruit, perhaps you can combine it with another; alternatively, you can substitute one fruit for another of similar structure and moisture content. Canned fruit *doesn't count unless you canned it yourself.* Think outside the box, use unconventional fruits, look to the natural world around you, and think about using fruits in season. Start a friendship with a fruit farmer—or two or three.

Bitters

We have a strong affection for using cocktail bitters in our recipes. We feel they add a special something, a secret ingredient if you will. If you can't find them at your local shops, look online; there are a variety of brands available by mail order, Fee Brothers and Angostura being some of the most common.

Honey

The same rule of thumb that we apply to fruit and dairy is true for honey: get it locally when you can. Find a beekeeper or go to a specialty shop and get your hands on honey that is produced in your region—or choose a specialty honey that comes from another area but is not from a factory. Commercially blended honeys (the label will usually read "Product of U.S.A. and Canada") really do not taste as good and will negatively affect the pie's flavor.

Maple Syrup

Use only fresh, 100 percent pure maple syrup. We like to source from Poorfarm Farm, along with a few other local producers, and if you can find Grade B, that's great. It's a little cheaper than Grade A and has a stronger maple flavor. Please do not use any sort of imitation maple syrup.

Molasses

We love molasses for its bitter, bold, and rich flavor. It is a unique sweetener that works great in many recipes. If you find yourself without brown sugar, all you need to do is add molasses to white sugar (1 tablespoon molasses per cup of sugar), and voilà, it's the same thing. We use good old-fashioned Grandma's molasses, which is readily available in most grocery stores.

Barley Malt Syrup

Barley malts are an unexpected ingredient for pie making. We add barley malt syrup to our pecan pie along with some dark chocolate, but you can also add it to cookies, cakes, and other baked goods when you are looking for that malty flavor. Our neighbor Brooklyn Homebrew is a great online source for it. We use their Briess Traditional Dark Liquid Malt Extract. Eden Foods also makes a good organic syrup that is easy to find online.

Spices

We use a variety of spices in this book. The most important thing to consider when selecting spices is freshness. If you want to grind your own using a mortar and pestle, that is awesome. If you prefer to buy your spices already ground, just be sure they are not old on the shelf, and don't keep them in your cupboard for years on end. Use them!

Demerara or Raw Sugar

We like to sprinkle raw sugar on double-crust or lattice pies after applying the egg wash and before baking. It is a matter of preference, but we like the way it looks and the extra little sweet crunch it gives to the crust. Sugar in the Raw or Billington's are good brands of this type of sugar and should be easy to find in your supermarket or specialty foods store.

Thickening Starches: Arrowroot, Tapioca, Potato, Flour, and Corn

Our favorite thickeners are arrowroot and potato starch. Bob's Red Mill is a readily available brand in most grocery stores and online. For apple fillings we simply use flour. Some fruits, such as berries and cherries, require a little more starch to help the filling to set, while apples are very high in pectin and require only flour to thicken their juices. Tapioca starch is also a good thickener but may be hard to come by; you can also grind tapioca pearls into powder in your mortar and pestle if you fancy. Cornstarch is a fine substitute for any of these starches; however, it is our least preferred, as we find it to be more gummy and tacky than the other starches.

Citrus Juices

For recipes that call for citrus juice, use freshly squeezed juice that you have prepared yourself from a fresh piece of citrus. It tastes so much better than shelf-stable bottled juice. Honestly, it's not even worth making the pie if you don't use fresh juice.

Salts: Sea Salt, Kosher Salt, and Table Salt

Natural sea salts are by far our favorite salts to use. The family-owned English salt company Maldon produces a delicious and relatively easy-to-find sea salt. It is what we (and most chefs) use for finishing; anything with "salted," "salty," or "salt" in the name is likely finished with Maldon. Otherwise, kosher salt is what you want to use when salt is called for in a filling and flake sea salt is not noted. Regular table salt will work if that's all you've got.

Corn Syrup

Corn syrup is not made by the devil, and just to clarify, we are not talking about high-fructose corn syrup (which is in fact a rather devilish product when added to all variety of commercial foods and beverages). We are talking about plain old-fashioned corn syrup. The one most commonly on the grocery shelf is Karo brand. They make a light version and a dark version; we use both in our recipes.

Sourcing

Farmers' Markets

In the busy months of fruit season we visit our local greenmarkets up to three times a week to get the freshest fruit for our pies. Our absolute favorite orchard to source from is Wilklow Orchards, but we also purchase from any other farmers that have beautiful products. Some of our favorites who sell their produce in Brooklyn include Bradley Farm, Evolutionary Organics, Lucky Dog Farm, Phillips Farms, and Toigo Orchards. Another very special market in New York City is the Amsterdam Market in the old Fulton Fish Market in downtown Manhattan. Maggie Nesciur of Flying Fox is there regularly with a selection of beautiful hand-picked fruits that we love to work with as well.

Foraged

Some of our most offbeat ingredients come from the wild. We wish we had the time to get out and forage for ourselves, but we don't. Instead we are lucky enough to work with Evan Strusinski, a talented East Coast forager who provides fresh-picked and unique ingredients to a great variety of food businesses in New York City. You'd be surprised what you can find in the wild that is totally edible and definitely delicious. Seek out a foraging community in your area, or purchase books on the subject in order to educate yourself about what grows in your region and when.

Online Sources

Bob's Red Mill (www.bobsredmill.com)

With products available both online and in grocery stores, this is a great source for potato starch and ground arrowroot.

Brooklyn Homebrew (www.brooklyn-homebrew.com)

We are lucky enough to have these knowledgeable neighbors and friends of the pie shop—they also sell all their products online. We use the Briess Traditional Dark Liquid Malt Extract for our Malted Chocolate Pecan Pie.

Right: Wild ginger root, freshly picked.

Opposite: The Wilklow family farm has been in operation since 1855. They provide us with a great variety of fruit and apples year round.

Frontier Natural Products Co-op
(www.frontiercoop.com)

For a great source of organic spices, visit their website. You can order online or look for their products in your local supermarket or health food store.

Hammons Black Walnuts
(www.black-walnuts.com)

Unless you have a tree full of them, black walnuts can be hard to find. This is a great online source for very fresh black walnuts.

Mymouné
(www.mymoune.com)

This family company from Lebanon carries lovely rose syrup and rose water, as well as other fruit and floral oils.

Poorfarm Farm
(www.poorfarmfarm.com)

This ninety-acre wooded farm in Vermont produces maple syrup the old-fashioned way, by gathering the sap in buckets and using the farm's own firewood to fuel the cooking. The result is a particularly delicious syrup that is perfect for baking.

Terra Spice Company
(www.terraspicecompany.com)

This is an excellent online source for high quality spices, spice blends, extracts, salts, and more.

Webstaurant
(www.webstaurantstore.com)

Webstaurant is an awesome resource for commercial kitchen tools that you can use at home. They also carry Angostura bitters.

Four generations of fruit farmers: Albert, Bill, Hank, and Fred Wilklow.

Tools

You don't have to spend a ton of money and time shopping for all the finest kitchen tools in order to make a good pie. However, investing in tools that you like and that hold up over time will help you get the job done easily and enjoyably. It is beyond frustrating to try to work with a subpar tool that falls apart halfway through whatever process you are in.

Understand how to use your tools and how to repair them if possible. (We are constantly wearing out and repairing our apple peelers, creating Frankenstein peelers by transferring pieces from one to another.) As relatively DIY, self-taught bakers, we have always been interested in learning about and investing in well-made kitchen tools. That said, we like to streamline (we get rid of unused or inferior tools on a regular basis) and keep our tool inventory down to only what is necessary.

Rolling Pin

Rolling pins can be a matter of preference. We agree that a well-balanced tapered (often called French-style) pin is the easiest to work with for rolling out pie dough. When working in a large kitchen, using a long pin with a large circumference can make quick work of the rolling process, but a tapered pin allows for versatility and precision when rolling—especially on a small countertop. A marble pin is nice in the summer; you can chill it in the freezer and have a cool tool to work your quickly softening pie dough; however, marble pins are quite heavy, and not all are created equal. If you choose marble, make sure the handles that hold the supporting rod through the middle are constructed well or it will fall apart quickly, and frustratingly, with use.

Handheld Pastry Blender

Disclaimer: we are not being paid to say this, but OXO makes the absolute best handheld pastry blender on the market, no question. We have bent and beaten up many a handheld pastry blender (not to mention our hands) trying to make crust with a cheap or poorly made version. OXO got it right. Buy the blade-style blender and you'll never need another.

Measuring Cups

Measuring cups come in two forms: those intended for liquid ingredients (designed to be easy to pour from) and those intended for dry ingredients (designed to be easy to level off). Get yourself a good Pyrex 1-cup or 4-cup measure for your liquids, and a simple metal set of four various-size cups for your dry ingredients.

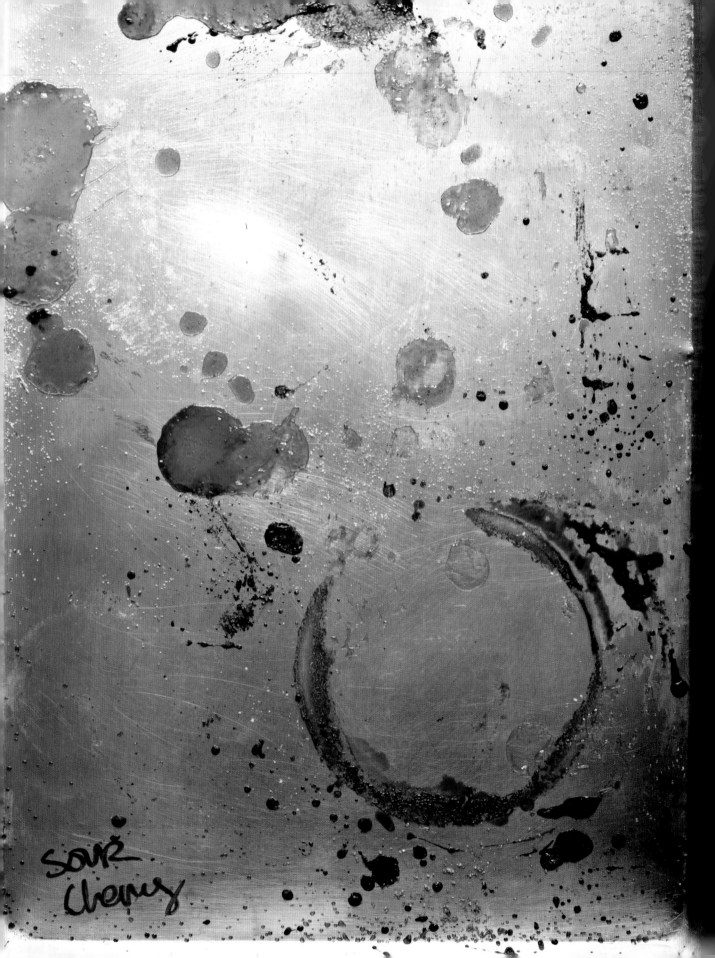

sour
Cherry

Measuring Spoons

Get yourself a full set of basic stainless steel measuring spoons, very simple, very necessary.

Pie Pans

The best all-purpose pie pan is a 9-inch Pyrex glass pan. Glass distributes heat evenly and the clear glass makes it possible to check the browning progress of the bottom crust. That said, we also use reusable aluminum pans in the shop on a regular basis. We find them especially suited to crumb crusts, as the rougher material seems to grab the crumbs, making pressing in easier. **A note about temperatures:** all temperatures given in this book are for baking in a glass pie pan unless otherwise noted. If using a metal pan, lower the temperature by 25°F, as metal conducts heat more quickly but less evenly than glass.

Tart Pans

There are a variety of shapes and sizes of tart pans on the market, and it is fun to stock your kitchen with some options. We suggest 9- or 10-inch round pans for the recipes in this book, as they are comparable to pie-pan size. We like the traditional, shiny, tin-plated, French-made pans; just be sure to dry them well after washing, as they are quick to tarnish.

Springform Pans

A standard springform pan works great for pie making. It gives you a straight (rather than slanted) crust edge and is a departure from the traditional ruffled tart-pan edge. Buy a good, sturdy pan with a well-constructed locking mechanism.

Food Processor

We don't suggest using a food processor for making a single batch of piecrust, but we do use one for quickly chopping all sorts of things and for blending herb and spice sugars. Even a 2-cup processor works great for most of these recipes if you don't want to give up storage space for the big one. However, if you want to make triple or quadruple batches of crust, using a large food processor to cut your butter and dry ingredients together is acceptable—but please, finish it by hand!

Immersion Blender

The immersion blender is an excellent and useful tool for pureeing your custards to a creamy and smooth consistency; you can use one to mix any of the custard recipes in this book. Get a small one and keep it in a drawer; you can make soups and smoothies with it too.

Baking Sheets

Standard, rimmed baking sheets (18 inches x 13 inches) are the easiest to work with. We like to use the same commercial baking sheets at home that we use in the pie shop because they are sturdy and reliable, not flimsy or prone to warping. They are much easier to handle going in and coming out of the oven and prevent overflowing filling from burning on the bottom of the oven (a mistake you will make only once).

Crust Shield

A crust shield is intended to prevent the crimped edge of a pie from becoming too dark and is typically used during the second half or so of total baking time. It allows you to keep the temperature high throughout to ensure the bottom crust will be nicely browned. It looks a lot like the outer ring of a tart pan, which is, in fact, exactly what we use for this purpose. You can purchase one if you like, or you can flip an appropriately sized tart ring over onto your crust to protect it once it has reached the desired level of browning. A temporary shield can also be fashioned by shaping aluminum foil into a ring.

Rubber Scrapers

Stock your kitchen with a couple of sizes of rubber scraper and at least one heatproof version. This is one of the most obvious and handy tools you can have for scraping the bowl clean and for easily mixing together textured fillings.

Wooden Spoons

In general, wooden spoons are preferable to metal, unless you're tasting something. We like to collect handmade, sturdy, long-handled wooden spoons for stirring up big batches of fillings—just be sure to keep the spoons you use for sweet preparations separate from the spoons you use for savory preparations to avoid adding a garlicky note to your peaches.

Whisks

We mostly use just two types of whisks in the pie shop: piano and French. A French whisk adds air when whipping cream and other things you want to aerate. A piano whisk is sturdier; it also adds a little air but it is more of a blending tool.

Mixing Bowls

Have a few sizes on hand: small, medium, and large. Lightweight metal bowls are the easiest to handle and to clean. For making crusts, a flat-bottomed bowl is best.

Bench Scraper

A bench scraper is absolutely necessary for making piecrust and an awesome tool for helping with counter cleanup. Get one and get in the habit of using it for everything, not just piecrust.

Ceramic Baking Beads

These little ceramic beads go into your foil-lined prebake to help hold the crust in place so it will not melt down into a puddle of butter and flour. You can easily use beans instead of beads, but the beads are pretty handy to have around.

Marble or Wood Slab

Wood is more forgiving and lightweight to move around, but marble is great for its ability to remain cool and for its nice smooth surface—we think it's a matter of preference and kitchen storage space.

Cherry Pitter

There are a few types on the market; we really like the old-fashioned handheld paper-punch style, but we also recently discovered the mason-jar-lid style—it's a stamp-down punch that is affixed to the lid of a mason jar (photo opposite), and we love it.

Mechanical Apple Peeler

We find the fastest way to prep apples for pies is to use a hand-crank peeler. It costs about twenty dollars and can cut apple prep time in half. We prefer the thin slices it creates, instead of wedges.

Pastry Brush

We recommend a fine-bristled silicone pastry brush with a metal handle. This style is easy to wash and will not fall apart.

Pizza Cutter

The pizza cutter is our favorite tool for cutting lattice. We don't see the point of messing with anything else, and it's also handy to have around for cutting pizza.

Timer

This one is sort of obvious. Having a timer is necessary for baking custards; 1 minute too long can make all the difference in texture and can result in cracking and overbrowning. Fruit pies are a lot more forgiving and give good visual cues as to when they are done if you pay attention, but you still want to keep a timer on them for rotation from the bottom of the oven to the top.

Knives

We don't keep a lot of fancy knives in our kitchen, really just the basics: a good 8- to 10-inch chef's knife, a decent long-blade serrated knife (or bread knife), and a variety of small paring knives. Victorinox makes quality kitchen knives at an affordable price with easy-to-clean handles. We are guilty of letting our knives get shamefully dull, but we are lucky to have our friend and neighborhood knife maker Joel Bukiewicz of Cut Brooklyn rescue us— he sharpens our knives for us in return for a double espresso or a slice of pie. If you are looking to invest in an outstanding, one-of-a-kind, handmade knife, you must visit his shop or his website: www.cutbrooklyn.com.

Techniques

When it comes to pie, technique is pretty important. Like most techniques, those for pie definitely have some variables and are honed over time. Here we've given you some advice and ideas based on what we've learned from others and what we've developed in our own kitchen.

Making the Crust

GETTING ORGANIZED

BUTTER

Opposite: Cutting butter with a bench scraper.

Piecrust making is a very personal thing. We always say that we can tell who made a batch of crust just by looking at it, and for the most part, that's true. The largest part of it is feel, but you must use technique to get that feel down. Always have all your ingredients ready. Have your ice water mixture ready; cube your butter and set it back in the fridge to stay cool until you need it. Measure out your flour and sugar and salt. Use a flat-bottomed bowl, which will give you stability. Use a good-quality pastry blender so you don't get frustrated with a broken or inferior tool.

Toss together the flour, sugar, and salt in a large, flat-bottomed bowl. Grab your pastry blender and just give it a mix. Toss in the cubed butter chunks and use the bench scraper to start cutting the butter into the flour mixture. Then, using the pastry blender, cut everything together until it begins to reach a cornmeal-like consistency—leaving a few small chunks of butter. Add half the ice water mixture and begin to fold it in with the pastry blender. The dough will still be dry and just beginning to come together. Add the rest of the ice water mixture and bring everything together with your hands. Don't be afraid to run your fingers through the crust a time or two (but no more than that or you may overwork it) to help create a marbleized effect with the butter through the flour mixture—do not, however, knead it like bread dough. The crust should *not* have large chunks of unblended butter. It should have streaks of butter.

The crust should be wrapped in plastic and put in the refrigerator to rest for at least half an hour before rolling out. It also works to freeze the crust if it's made long in advance of use; just be sure to wrap it well in plastic wrap. It will keep for about a month.

Use a handheld pastry blender to cut the butter into the dry ingredients.

Fully incorporated butter, flour, salt, and sugar will look like this.

Use your hands to bring the dough together after adding the water mixture.

The dough should be marbleized with streaks of butter.

Rolling Out the Dough

Remove the dough from the fridge 5 to 10 minutes before you begin rolling. Dough that is too cold will develop cracks when it is rolled.

Lightly flour your work surface and a French (tapered) rolling pin. (If you're not using a French rolling pin, follow the instructions in the next paragraph for using a flat rolling pin.) Place the dough in the center of the work surface, and beginning from slightly below the center of the disc, roll the dough away from you using one even stroke, applying more pressure on the left side of the pin than on the right; most of the flattening will occur in the upper-left quadrant of the dough circle. Decrease pressure as you reach the dough's edge. After each stroke, spin the disc an eighth to a quarter turn counterclockwise and roll again. Sprinkle more flour underneath and on top of the dough and on the rolling pin as you work; use just enough to prevent the dough from sticking.

As the disc becomes larger, use care to not overstretch the center of the dough. The tapered-style rolling pin tends to put more pressure on the center of the disc, so once the dough circle is 8 to 9 inches across, we like to switch to a flat pin to finish rolling (either handled or dowel-type; if you prefer this type overall, your rollout instructions start here). Continue rolling in the same fashion as before, starting just below the center of the disc and pushing away from you, but now apply even pressure across the entire top half of the disc, lightening up as you reach the dough's edge; then rotate counterclockwise. If cracks develop, cut a piece of dough from the edge and pat it into the crack to patch (you can also add a brush of water to help seal it if needed).

Roll the dough until it is 2 to 3 inches larger than the pan you are using and about ⅛ inch in thickness.

If you want to do this step ahead of time, you can roll out the dough into a flat disc, place it on a sheet of parchment paper that is larger than the disc, and then gently roll it up. Freeze the dough solid, then wrap it tightly in plastic wrap, and put it back in the freezer until you need it. Allow it to thaw until pliable, about 15 minutes, before using.

Roll outward and decrease pressure as you reach the dough's edge.

Fitting Dough for a Pie Pan

Fold the dough disc in half and lay it across one side of a well-buttered pie pan, positioning the seam in the center. Unfold the disc and gently slide and fit the dough down into the pan; do not pull or stretch the dough. Make sure there are no gaps between the dough and the pan; if there are air bubbles, burst them with a fork.

Trim the dough overhang to allow 1 to 1½ inches of excess, measuring from the inner rim of the pan. Cover the crust with plastic and refrigerate for at least 30 minutes, preferably 1 hour or more, and tightly wrapped, up to 3 days before using. The rolled out, fitted, tightly wrapped crust can also be frozen for up to a month.

Fitting Dough for a Tart or Springform Pan

Place the pan in the middle of the dough disc, and using a pastry wheel, trim the dough into a circle at least 1½ inches larger around than the pan bottom if using a springform pan, or 2 inches larger around than the pan bottom if using a tart pan.

Butter the pan thoroughly. Separate the pan base from the pan ring (if using a springform pan, leave the latch open). Fold the dough disc in half and lay it across one side of the pan base. Unfold the disc so that it is centered over the base. Pick up the pan ring, bring your hand through its bottom, and hang it on your forearm. Using the same hand, pick up the dough-lined pan base and position it on your fingertips. Guide the pan ring up with the opposite hand while lowering the base and crust to fit inside. Place the pan on a flat surface (if using a springform, close the latch). Gently finish sliding and pushing the dough down the pan sides until it is settled into the corners (where the side meets the bottom) of the pan; do not pull or stretch the dough. Make sure there are no gaps between the dough and the pan.

If using a springform pan, the dough may come only partway up the side of the pan, depending on the height of the pan. The shell should have only about 1½-inch-high sides when finished.

For a tart pan, fold the excess dough overhang to the inside of the shell to reinforce just the sides, and press to seal. Trim off the crust that remains extended beyond the top of the pan by pressing down and out with your thumb and using the pan edge to pinch it off.

If the dough is to be prebaked, prick the sides and bottom about 15 times with a fork. This allows the crust to "breathe" a little by letting steam escape from within while it is baking, which prevents shrinking. Cover the crust with plastic and refrigerate for at least 30 minutes, preferably 1 hour or more, and tightly wrapped, up to 3 days before using. The rolled out, fitted, tightly wrapped crust can also be frozen for up to a month.

Cutting and Weaving Lattice

Throughout this book you will see different examples of lattice widths and weaving, including braiding. Lattice can be cut into any width you desire. Be creative with shapes and sizes. There are just a couple of things to remember: it's much easier to work with the dough when it is well chilled, and a pizza cutter is the easiest tool to use for cutting lattice strips. The following directions are for a pie with a total of 8 strips of lattice.

A: On a floured surface, roll the prepared dough into a circle approximately 12 inches in diameter and about ⅛-inch thick, following the directions provided under "Rolling Out the Dough" on page 54.

B: Using a pizza cutter, trim one inch of dough from either side of the disc to square off the circle; discard the trimmings.

C: Cut the remaining shape into 8 strips of equal width. This is your lattice. Transfer the lattice to a parchment-lined (or flour-dusted) baking sheet and chill for a minimum of 30 minutes.

To weave the lattice:

D: Lay strip number 1 of the lattice vertically across the top of the filled pie, just slightly to the left of the center. Lay strip number 2 over strip number 1 at a 90 degree angle, just below the center of the pie. Lay strip 3 over strip 2 to the right of and parallel to strip 1. **E:** Lay strip 4 over strip 2 to the left of and parallel to strip 1. **F:** Fold back the right end of strip 2, and lay strip 5 to the right of and parallel to strip 3. **G:** Unfold strip 2 so it's on top of strip 5, completing your vertical lattice placement.

H: Fold back the top ends of strips 1 and 5, and lay strip 6 above and parallel to strip 2. **I:** Return the top ends of strips 1 and 5 to their original positions. Fold back the bottoms of strips 1 and 5, and lay strip 7 below and parallel to strip 2. **J:** Return the bottom ends of strips 1 and 5 to their original positions. Fold back the top ends of strips 3 and 4, and lay strip 8 above and parallel to strip 6.

K: Return strips 3 and 4 to their original positions. Your pie is now ready to be crimped. For instructions on crimping, see "Assembling and Crimping Fruit Pies" on page 64.

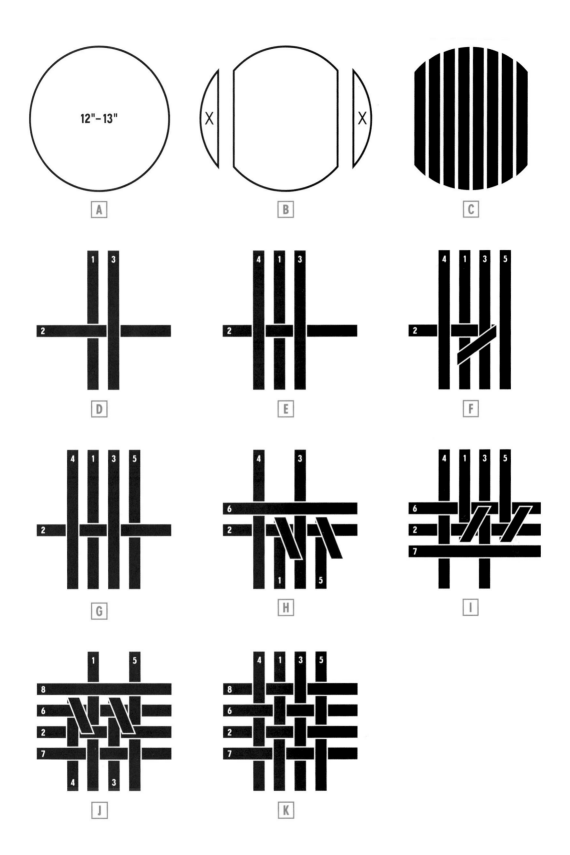

Use a pizza cutter to accurately and evenly portion lattice strips.

A bench scraper is helpful for transferring cut lattice to a parchment-lined baking sheet.

Placement of the first lattice strip (off center).

Weave the lattice according to the instructions on page 58.

Crimping for Single-Crust Pies

As with many aspects of pie making, how you crimp (or flute) the outer edge is a matter of personal style and preference. We have found that as a rule, it's best to roll the excess dough overhang under when preparing to crimp a single-crust pie (such as a custard, which generally requires a prebaked crust). Rolling the excess dough overhang inward is easier when preparing to crimp a lattice- or full-topped pie.

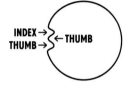

To prepare the fitted, trimmed dough of a single-crust pie for crimping, roll and pinch the excess dough edge under so that it sits directly on top of the pan's rim. Do not be afraid to pinch tightly; otherwise, the crust may unravel while baking. If your fingers are sticking to the dough, dust them with a little extra flour. Continue to roll and pinch the dough all the way around the circumference of the pan until you have created a "wall" of dough that can be shaped and fluted. Next, use the index finger and thumb of one hand to create a letter C that the thumb of your opposite hand fits perfectly into. Hold this C at the outside of the crust "wall" and push inward while simultaneously pushing your opposite thumb into the center of the C from the inside of the crust "wall." Use this as your mold to crimp the edges of the pie all the way around, making sure the final fluted crust sits directly on top of the pan's rim. See the photo on page 65 for a clear illustration. Alternatively, for an easier crust edge style, you can use the tines of a fork to press the dough wall flat down onto the pie pan rim (see the image for Lavender Honey Custard Pie on page 87).

Assembling and Crimping Fruit Pies

We like to sprinkle the bottom of a fruit pie shell with 1 teaspoon each flour and granulated sugar before pouring in the filling; this mixture acts as an absorbent layer to suck up some of the excess juice, thereby helping to make a crisper bottom crust.

When filling a fruit pie, you want to be certain you fill it enough, but be careful to not overfill it. For juicy fillings, such as blueberry, fill just to the top of the pan. Drier fillings, such as apple, can be mounded in the center. A fruit pie will be topped with lattice, a full-top crust, or a crumble or streusel topping. For streusel or crumble, you can use the crimping technique explained in "Crimping for Single-Crust Pies," above.

Crimp your way around the pie using both thumbs and your index finger.

For lattice- or full-topped fruit pies, prepare the crust for crimping by rolling and pinching the excess dough overhang inward so it makes a crust "wall" that just sits on top of the pan rim, incorporating the top pastry round or lattice as you go. Next, use the index finger and thumb of one hand to create a letter C that the thumb of your opposite hand fits perfectly into. Hold this C at the outside of the crust "wall" and push inward while simultaneously pushing your opposite thumb into the center of the C from the inside of the crust "wall." Use this as your mold to crimp the edges of the pie all the way around, making sure the final fluted crust sits directly on top of the pan's rim.

Cut a few vents in a full-topped pie to allow steam to escape while baking.

Develop your own crimping style. It's your signature.

Shaping a Galette

We consider galettes a part of the extended pie family—pie's cool older cousin, perhaps. They are fun and easy to make with piecrust, require no pie pan, and are the perfect solution when you have a small amount of a certain fruit or when you want a small dessert.

To shape a galette is not difficult. There are a few key things to remember: (1) do not overfill the galette with the filling or it will collapse, and (2) chill the galette very well before baking. We usually like to start with the dough in a large circular shape; sprinkle it with a little sugar and flour; place the filling in the middle and allow it to spread out a little, about 3 inches from the edge; and then fold the edges in, crimping the dough tightly to itself in a circle, almost creating a little satchel, but leaving an opening in the center. The galette will inevitably leak some filling onto the tray, but baking on parchment paper or a silicone baking mat (such as Silpat) will help make cleanup easy.

You can also cut decorative edges into your galette. The main thing to consider is the symmetry of the pattern, which will determine how the edges will fold in. For example, in the Lemon Verbena Raspberry Galette (see page 97), we cut triangle shapes all around an ample center circle, creating a sort of star whose points could be folded in. For the Gooseberry Galette (see page 140), we used a biscuit cutter to create a flower shape with a circle in the center and petals that are evenly spaced and folded in. Be creative in how you shape your galette; it is, after all, by definition a free-form pastry.

Prebaking

When baking custard, cream, or other liquid-based pie fillings, you often need to give the crust a baking head start to ensure that it spends enough time in the oven overall. This step is called prebaking, or blind baking. The pie shell is lined with foil, and a heat-conductive material (pie weights or beans, for example) stands in for the filling; without this replacement, the dough will melt down into the pan and you won't be baking pie any longer. With it, you'll have a crisp, flaky crust to offset your perfectly textured buttermilk chess, or sweet corn custard, or buttered rum cream, or…

Have your crust rolled, crimped, and rested in the refrigerator for at least 30 minutes. When it's fully chilled, use a fork to prick all over the bottom and sides, 15 to 20 times. This step, called docking, helps eliminate the air bubbles that can form when the dough is exposed to heat and also prevents the crust from shrinking. Place the crust in the freezer.

Position the oven racks in the bottom and center positions, place a rimmed baking sheet on the lowest rack, and preheat the oven to 425°F. Have ready 1 egg white whisked with 1 teaspoon of water to brush the crust with during baking. This glaze acts to moistureproof the bottom and sides of the crust that will be exposed to the filling. It's not totally necessary but does make for a better final product.

When the crust is frozen solid (about 10 minutes), line it tightly with a piece or two of aluminum foil. Make sure the crimped edges are completely covered and there are no gaps between the foil and the crust.

Partial Prebaking: For Fillings That Will Be Baked

Pour the pie weights or beans into the pan and spread them so they are concentrated more around the edge of the shell than in the center. Place the pan on the preheated baking sheet and bake for 20 minutes, until the crimped edges are set but not browned.

Remove the pan and the baking sheet from the oven, lift out the foil and pie weights, and let the crust cool for a minute. Use a pastry brush to coat the bottom and sides with a thin layer of egg white glaze (1 egg white whisked with 1 teaspoon of water) to moistureproof the crust. Return the pan, on the baking sheet, to the oven's middle rack and continue baking for 3 more minutes. Remove and cool completely before filling.

Full Prebaking: For Fillings That Are Fully Cooked

Pour the pie weights or beans into the pan and spread them so they are concentrated more around the edge of the shell than in the center. Place the pan on the preheated baking sheet and bake for 20 minutes.

Remove the pan and the baking sheet from the oven, lift out the foil and pie weights, and let the crust cool for a minute. Use a pastry brush to coat the bottom and sides with a thin layer of egg white glaze (1 egg white whisked with 1 teaspoon of water) to moistureproof the crust. Return the pan, on the baking sheet, to the oven's middle rack and continue baking for 8 to 10 more minutes, or until the crust is golden brown all over. Remove and cool completely before filling.

Finishing and Troubleshooting

If your crust develops holes on the bottom or sides while baking, patch them, when baking is done, with a small amount of raw dough while the crust is still hot from the oven. As the dough melts, you can spread it like putty to seal it to the baked crust.

If your crust shrinks, you may be able to reshape it if it hasn't fully set yet. While it is still hot, use a clean, folded kitchen towel to apply gentle, even pressure to the edges to push them back up and into place.

Baking Fruit Pies

Our favorite choice for glazing the top crust is a simple egg wash for the deep golden color it gives the baked crust. You can also use milk or cream or just leave the glaze off altogether. Sprinkling sugar on the top is also optional; we've found our customers like the little bit of texture and crunch that comes from a sprinkle of demerara sugar.

Baking on a rimmed baking sheet is a necessity—fill your kitchen with the smoke of burned butter just once and you'll know why. In a pinch, make a baking tray from aluminum foil with the edges folded up to catch runoff.

Starting the pie on the lowest rack of the oven helps to set the bottom crust and ensure proper and thorough browning. Moving to the middle rack partway through baking allows the top crust to brown evenly. If at any point the top crust is getting too dark, you can use a crust shield (see page 45) or lower the oven temperature to finish.

To tell if a pie is fully baked, look for the juices to be bubbling throughout and, if you are using a glass plate, pick it up to be sure the bottom is fully browned and not still pale and raw in the center. When baking an apple pie, test for doneness with a skewer—the apples should be soft but not mushy; you want them to maintain some structure.

Baking Custard Pies

Custard pies are by far more finicky and less forgiving than fruit pies. There is a finite window of time in which they must be removed from the oven; miss that window and you'll end up with either an underbaked, runny mess or an overcooked curdled filling. Practice makes perfect when working with custards, and even we miss the mark occasionally.

That said, there are a few cues you can look for to identify when a custard is perfectly cooked.

Generally, as it nears finishing, the outer 2 inches of the custard will be set and puffed up slightly, while the center will remain a liquid that will slosh a bit, independent of the outer ring, when the pan is shaken. At this point, check the pie's progress every 30 to 60 seconds.

When the center *just* changes from liquid to barely set, pull the pie from the oven. When the pan is lightly shaken, the filling should still be jiggly but moving as one. The residual heat will continue to cook the filling as it cools.

Check individual recipes for more specific instructions.

Let the Pie Cool Before You Slice It

It's no secret that the minute a fresh pie comes out of the oven, everyone wants a slice. You might be tempted to cut into that freshly baked, steaming-hot pie, but you'd do yourself and the pie a favor to let it cool before you do. Giving the pie ample cooling time, at least 1 hour, will yield a pie that slices and plates so much better than a pie straight out of the oven. You really do need to give all that delicious filling that you so attentively prepared some time to cool and set.

In the shop, we use slicing guides to slice our pies into six, seven, or eight slices. If you are going to be making a lot of pies and you want all your slices to be portioned exactly, you could purchase a slicing guide from a restaurant supplier, but more than likely you'll want to just slice the pie in as big or as small slices as your pie eaters request. We recommend using a serrated knife for fruit pies and a straight-bladed paring knife for custards. Slide the blade through the slice at least three times to ensure that you've gotten the crust sliced all the way through (and to avoid disaster when scooping it out for the plate). Use a traditional triangle-shaped pie server for ease in removing the slices from the pan—especially the first one!

Spring

Spring

Spring may not be the first season that comes to mind for pie making: fruit is in limited supply, citrus is waning, and herbs are just getting started. Yet we love this season for its feeling of renewal and light and its signs of the coming warmth. We aim to make our spring pies in that spirit.

This is the time of year that we get creative and often develop new custards or cream pies for the shop, somewhat because of the lack of ingredients to work with, but mostly to satisfy our creative desire for experimentation and lightening things up. When rhubarb arrives, we rejoice—finally something to work with other than eggs and cream. Next come strawberries, followed by sour cherries (a sure sign that summer is very close), and our hands stay busy chopping, hulling, and pitting into the night. When we receive first word from our forager Evan Strusinski, we look forward to what will be on the list of unique ingredients to work with for the season. Wild ginger is a favorite, and we love pairing it with strawberries and, later in the summer, stone fruits.

We are lucky to have talented rooftop farmer Frieda Lim as our neighbor. When we built our window boxes, Frieda came to the rescue with planting guidance and expertise, so we grow a large amount of herbs for our custard and fruit pies right outside our window.

Rhubarb Pie

Makes one 9-inch pie
Serves 8 to 10

As hard as it is for us to believe, "What's rhubarb?" is an often-asked question in the pie shop. Dubbed the "pie plant," rhubarb has a rich history in pie making and holds a special place in our hearts. We are always excited to introduce it to new customers at the pie shop. During our years growing up in South Dakota eating rhubarb was a highlight of the summer and the main ingredient in one of our favorite pies made by Grandma Liz. She did not combine her rhubarb with any berries—it was straight rhubarb and nothing else. Our recipe is based on her purist approach.

All-Butter Crust for a 9-inch double-crust pie (see page 207)

1½ to 2 pounds fresh rhubarb, cut into ½-inch pieces (5 to 6 cups) (frozen, thawed, and drained if desired)
¾ cup packed light brown sugar
½ cup granulated sugar
¼ teaspoon ground allspice
¼ teaspoon ground cardamom
¼ teaspoon ground ginger
½ teaspoon kosher salt
3 to 4 tablespoons ground arrowroot
1 tablespoon fresh lemon juice
1 large egg
Dash Angostura bitters
Egg wash (1 large egg whisked with 1 teaspoon water and a pinch of salt)
Demerara sugar, for finishing

If you have the time, wash, chop, and freeze your rhubarb at least one day before baking to help release excess moisture. Thaw in a strainer before using, but don't squeeze it or you might dry it out too much.

Have ready and refrigerated one pastry-lined 9-inch pie pan and pastry rounds or lattice to top (see pages 56 and 58).

Combine the rhubarb, brown and granulated sugars, allspice, cardamom, ginger, salt, and arrowroot in a large bowl and mix thoroughly. Stir in the lemon juice, egg, and bitters. Pour the filling into the refrigerated pie shell, arrange the lattice or pastry round on top, and crimp as desired (see pages 58 and 64).

Chill the pie in the refrigerator for 10 to 15 minutes to set the pastry. Meanwhile, position the oven racks in the bottom and center positions, place a rimmed baking sheet on the bottom rack, and preheat the oven to 425°F.

Brush the pastry with the egg wash to coat; if your pie has a lattice top, be careful not to drag the filling onto the pastry (it will burn). Sprinkle the pastry with the desired amount of demerara sugar.

Place the pie on the rimmed baking sheet on the lowest rack of the oven. Bake for 20 to 25 minutes, or until the pastry is set and beginning to brown. Lower the oven temperature to 375°F, move the pie to the center oven rack, and continue to bake until the pastry is a deep golden brown and the juices are bubbling throughout, 30 to 35 minutes longer.

Allow to cool completely on a wire rack, 2 to 3 hours. Serve slightly warm or at room temperature.

The pie will keep in the refrigerator for 3 days or at room temperature for 2 days.

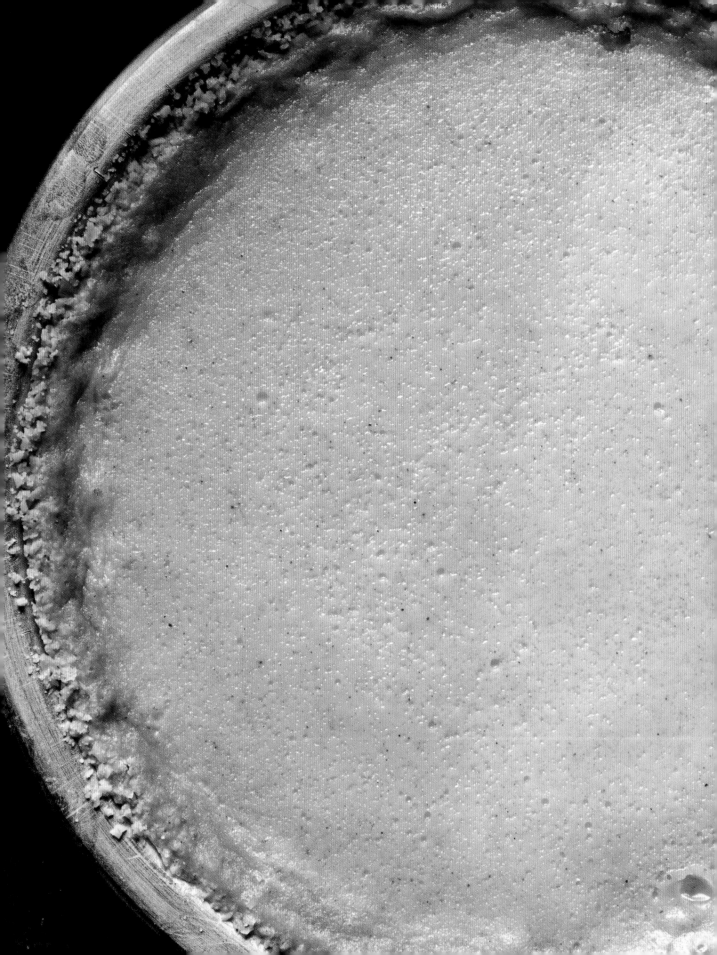

Rhubarb Custard Pie

One of our favorite rhubarb desserts, which were a mainstay of spring and summer in South Dakota, was rhubarb crisp. Fresh from the oven with a little evaporated milk or ice cream on top, it was the perfect balance of creaminess with the tart rhubarb and a hint of spice. This custard pie recipe is inspired by that combination; here the oats appear in the crust and the rhubarb is cooked into a compote so that the custard ever so lightly floats atop.

Makes one 9-inch pie
Serves 8 to 10

Oat Crumble Crust for a 9-inch single-crust pie (see page 216), prebaked

1 pound fresh rhubarb, chopped into 1-inch pieces (about 3 cups)
1¼ cups granulated sugar
3 tablespoons cornstarch
½ teaspoon kosher salt
¼ cup heavy cream
¾ cup sour cream
⅛ teaspoon fresh grated nutmeg
½ teaspoon vanilla paste (Nielsen-Massey makes a readily available one)
2 large eggs

We use our Oat Crumble Crust for this pie, but any of the crumb crusts (see page 209, 212, 214, 215, or 216) work well. Try different pairings.

Position a rack in the center of the oven and preheat the oven to 325°F. Place the prebaked pie shell on a rimmed baking sheet.

In a medium saucepan, combine the rhubarb, ¾ cup of the sugar, the cornstarch, and ¼ teaspoon of the salt. Cook over medium heat until the rhubarb is cooked down into a thick sauce. Set aside to cool while preparing the custard.

In a large bowl, combine the remaining ½ cup sugar, remaining ¼ teaspoon salt, heavy and sour creams, nutmeg, and vanilla paste, and mix until smooth. Stir in the eggs one at a time and mix well.

Spread the rhubarb mixture evenly in the prebaked crust. Strain the cream mixture through a fine-mesh sieve directly over the rhubarb or strain it into a separate bowl and then pour it over the rhubarb. Bake on the middle rack of the oven for 25 to 30 minutes, rotating 180 degrees when the edges start to set, about 15 minutes through baking. The pie is finished when the edges are set and puffed slightly and the center is no longer liquid but still quite wobbly. Be careful not to overbake or the custard can curdle and separate; the filling will continue to cook and set after the pie is removed from the oven. Allow to cool completely on a wire rack, 2 to 3 hours. Serve slightly warm, at room temperature, or cool.

The pie will keep refrigerated for 2 days or at room temperature for 1 day.

Strawberry Balsamic Pie

Makes one 9-inch pie
Serves 8 to 10

When Italian cooks first put aceto balsamico on fresh strawberries, they had the right idea—sweet, fragrant berries balanced by the earthy tartness of balsamic vinegar is a killer combination. We love our recipe for this pie—and it's one of our most popular in the shop.

All-Butter Crust for a 9-inch double-crust pie (see page 207)

Our friend and former pie shop baker and barista Sara Franklin likes to use the juice that drains off the strawberries by reducing it over low heat to make a syrup—it's great drizzled over yogurt or ice cream or mixed with seltzer.

¼ cup plus 3 tablespoons granulated sugar
2 pounds fresh strawberries, rinsed and quartered (5 to 6 cups)
1 small baking apple (such as Northern Spy or Golden Delicious)
2 tablespoons balsamic vinegar
2 dashes Angostura bitters
¾ cup packed light brown sugar
3 tablespoons ground arrowroot
2 grinds fresh black pepper, fine setting
½ teaspoon kosher salt
Egg wash (1 large egg whisked with 1 teaspoon water and a pinch of salt)
Demerara sugar, for finishing

Have ready and refrigerated one pastry-lined 9-inch pie pan and pastry round or lattice to top (see pages 56 and 58).

Sprinkle 3 tablespoons of the granulated sugar over the strawberries. Stir gently to combine and allow the fruit to macerate at room temperature for 30 minutes to 1 hour.

Peel the apple and shred on the large holes of a box grater. Drain the strawberries of excess liquid and combine with the shredded apple. Sprinkle on the balsamic vinegar and Angostura bitters.

In a separate bowl, mix together the remaining ¼ cup granulated sugar, brown sugar, arrowroot, black pepper, and salt. Gently fold the sugar mixture into the strawberry mixture. Pour the filling into the refrigerated pie shell, arrange the lattice or pastry round on top, and crimp as desired (see pages 58 and 64).

Chill the pie in the refrigerator for 10 to 15 minutes to set the pastry.

Meanwhile, position the oven racks at the bottom and center positions, place a rimmed baking sheet on the bottom rack, and preheat the oven to 425°F.

Brush the pastry with the egg wash; if your pie has a lattice top, be careful not to drag the filling onto the pastry (it will burn). Sprinkle with the desired amount of demerara sugar.

Place the pie on the rimmed baking sheet on the lowest rack of the oven. Bake for 20 to 25 minutes, or until the pastry is set and beginning to brown. Lower the oven temperature to 375°F, move the pie to the center oven rack, and continue to bake until the pastry is a deep golden brown and the juices are bubbling throughout, 35 to 40 minutes longer.

Allow to cool completely on a wire rack, 2 to 3 hours. Serve slightly warm or at room temperature.

The pie will keep refrigerated for 3 days or at room temperature for 2 days.

Wild Ginger Strawberry Pie

Makes one 9-inch pie
Serves 8 to 10

Wild ginger is a different species from traditional culinary ginger, and it has a beautiful roselike fragrance that pairs amazingly well with fruits—especially strawberry. Our wild ginger comes from Vermont, and is mailed to us each summer by our forager. It is labor-intensive to prep (use a vegetable peeler and rinse it well) but absolutely worth the effort for its unique and entirely unexpected flavor.

All-Butter Crust for a 9-inch double-crust pie (see page 207)

¼ cup plus 3 tablespoons granulated sugar
2 pounds fresh strawberries, rinsed and quartered (5 to 6 cups)
1 small baking apple (such as Northern Spy or Golden Delicious)
2 tablespoons fresh lemon juice
Dash Angostura bitters
½ cup packed light brown sugar
2 teaspoons minced wild ginger
3 to 4 tablespoons ground arrowroot
¼ teaspoon ground allspice
½ teaspoon kosher salt
Egg wash (1 large egg whisked with 1 teaspoon water and a pinch of salt)
Demerara sugar, for finishing

If you are unable to find or forage wild ginger, you can substitute with standard store-bought fresh ginger (not dried). It won't taste the same, but it will still be a killer pie. Use the same ratio of sugar to ginger.

Have ready and refrigerated one pastry-lined 9-inch pie pan and pastry round or lattice to top (see pages 56 and 58).

Sprinkle 3 tablespoons of the granulated sugar over the strawberries. Stir gently to combine and allow the fruit to macerate at room temperature for 30 minutes to 1 hour.

Peel the apple and shred on the large holes of a box grater. Drain the strawberries of excess liquid and combine with the shredded apple. Sprinkle on the lemon juice and Angostura bitters.

In a separate bowl, mix together the remaining ¼ cup granulated sugar, brown sugar, wild ginger, arrowroot, allspice, and salt. Gently fold the sugar mixture into the strawberry mixture. Pour the filling into the refrigerated pie shell, arrange the lattice or pastry round on top, and crimp as desired (see pages 58 and 64).

Chill the pie in the refrigerator for 10 to 15 minutes to set the pastry.

Meanwhile, position the oven racks in the bottom and center positions, place a rimmed baking sheet on the bottom rack, and preheat the oven to 425°F.

Brush the pastry with the egg wash; if your pie has a lattice top, be careful not to drag the filling onto the pastry (it will burn). Sprinkle with the desired amount of demerara sugar.

Place the pie on the rimmed baking sheet on the lowest rack of the oven. Bake for 20 to 25 minutes, or until the pastry is set and beginning to brown. Lower the oven temperature to 375°F, move the pie to the center oven rack, and continue to bake until the pastry is a deep golden brown and the juices are bubbling throughout, 35 to 40 minutes longer.

Allow to cool completely on a wire rack, 2 to 3 hours. Serve slightly warm or at room temperature.

The pie will keep refrigerated for 3 days or at room temperature for 2 days.

Chamomile Buttermilk Custard Pie

Makes one 9-inch pie
Serves 8 to 10

When cold weather finally breaks and spring is in the air, our palates crave lighter flavors. The combination of floral chamomile and tangy buttermilk makes for a perfectly light springtime pie.

All-Butter Crust for a 9-inch single-crust pie (see page 207), partially prebaked (see page 68)

To infuse the chamomile in this recipe, you will essentially be making a tea with heated cream and dried chamomile.

1 cup heavy cream

3 chamomile teabags, or 3 tablespoons dried chamomile flowers

4 tablespoons (½ stick) unsalted butter, melted

¾ cup granulated sugar

½ teaspoon kosher salt

1 tablespoon all-purpose flour

3 large eggs

1 large egg yolk

1 cup buttermilk

1 tablespoon white vinegar

Position a rack in the center of the oven and preheat the oven to 325°F. Place the prebaked pie shell on a rimmed baking sheet.

In a medium heavy-bottomed saucepan, bring the heavy cream just to a boil over medium heat. Remove the cream from the heat, add the teabags or chamomile flowers, cover, and set aside to steep for at least 10 minutes.

Meanwhile, whisk together the melted butter, sugar, salt, and flour in a large bowl. Stir in the eggs one at a time, then the yolk. Remove the teabags from the cream, or strain the cream through a fine-mesh sieve. Add the buttermilk and white vinegar to the chamomile cream, and then slowly stream the cream mixture into the egg mixture.

Strain the filling through a fine-mesh sieve directly into the pie shell, or strain it into a separate bowl and then pour it into the shell. Bake on the middle rack of the oven for 45 to 50 minutes, rotating 180 degrees when the edges start to set, 30 to 35 minutes through baking. The pie is finished when the edges are set and puffed slightly and the center is no longer liquid but still quite wobbly. Be careful not to overbake or the custard can separate; the filling will continue to cook and set after the pie is removed from the oven. Allow to cool completely on a wire rack, 2 to 3 hours. Serve slightly warm, at room temperature, or cool.

The pie will keep refrigerated for 2 days or at room temperature for 1 day.

Lavender Honey Custard Pie

Makes one 9-inch pie
Serves 8 to 10

This custard looks and tastes like a warm and sunny spring day. Feel free to try different types of floral honey in this recipe, such as orange blossom, dandelion, or linden.

All-Butter Crust for a 9-inch single-crust pie (see page 207), partially prebaked (see page 68)

The recipe for candied lavender flowers will provide more than you need for this pie; save them in an airtight container (in the freezer or cupboard) and sprinkle on cakes, cookies, and breads.

⅓ cup granulated sugar
1 tablespoon flour
1 tablespoon stone-ground white cornmeal
½ teaspoon kosher salt
3 tablespoons unsalted butter, melted
⅔ cup lavender honey (or any variety floral honey)
3 large eggs, lightly beaten
1 large egg yolk
1½ cups heavy cream
2 teaspoons fresh lemon juice
4 drops food-grade lavender oil
Candied lavender flowers, to garnish (recipe follows)

Position a rack in the center of the oven and preheat the oven to 325°F. Place the prebaked pie shell on a rimmed baking sheet.

In a large bowl, whisk together the sugar, flour, cornmeal, and salt. Whisk in the melted butter, followed by the honey. Add the eggs and egg yolk one at a time, whisking well after each addition. Add the heavy cream, lemon juice, and lavender oil, and whisk well to combine.

Strain the filling through a fine-mesh sieve directly into the pie shell, or strain it into a separate bowl and then pour it into the shell. Bake on the middle rack of the oven for 40 to 50 minutes, rotating 180 degrees when the edges start to set, 30 to 35 minutes through baking. The pie is finished when the edges are set and puffed slightly and the center is no longer liquid but still quite wobbly. Be careful not to overbake or the custard can separate; the filling will continue to cook and set after the pie is removed from the oven. Allow to cool completely on a wire rack, 2 to 3 hours. Serve slightly warm, at room temperature, or cool.

The pie will keep refrigerated for 2 days or at room temperature for 1 day.

Candied Lavender Flowers

3 tablespoons dried lavender flowers
1 teaspoon water
1 tablespoon granulated sugar

Line a baking sheet with parchment paper and preheat the oven to 200°F.

Pour the lavender flowers into a small bowl, sprinkle with the water, and fluff with a fork to distribute the water evenly. Pour the moistened lavender flowers into a 6-inch or larger fine-mesh sieve and shake off any excess water. Sprinkle the sugar, ½ teaspoon at a time, over the flowers, shaking to distribute the sugar in between additions. Tap the sieve firmly against the heel of your hand to shake off excess sugar. Spread the flowers evenly on the prepared baking sheet and place in the oven to dry for 20 minutes. Cool, and then break up any clumps with your fingertips.

Candied flowers will keep indefinitely in an airtight container.

Lizzie's Lemon Sour Cream Pie

Makes one 9-inch pie
Serves 8 to 10

Our grandmother's cream pies were some of our favorites as kids. If she ever had too much filling for the pie, she would set it aside in a bowl for us to have as an after-school snack. This recipe is based on one of her classic cream pies—our favorite.

All-Butter Crust for a 9-inch single-crust pie (see page 207), fully prebaked (see page 69)

Grate fresh lemon zest on top of the fresh whipped cream immediately before serving to add a bright note—if you do it too long before serving, it will dry up and look unpleasant.

2½ cups sour cream
½ cup whole milk
1 cup granulated sugar
2 tablespoons plus 2 teaspoons cornstarch
½ teaspoon kosher salt
Zest of 2 lemons
¼ teaspoon orange zest (from about ¼ orange)
5 tablespoons fresh lemon juice (from about 3 lemons)
4 large egg yolks
4 tablespoons (½ stick) unsalted butter
1 cup heavy cream
2 tablespoons confectioners' sugar
½ teaspoon vanilla extract

In a large heavy-bottomed saucepan, whisk together the sour cream, milk, granulated sugar, cornstarch, salt, zests, and lemon juice. Bring to a boil over medium heat, stirring occasionally. Reduce the heat to medium-low and continue to simmer for 2 minutes longer, stirring constantly. Then remove it from the heat.

Have ready a fine-mesh sieve positioned on the rim of a large bowl. Whisk the yolks in a small bowl. Slowly whisk in about 1 cup of the hot lemon mixture to temper the yolks. Add the yolk mixture back to the saucepan, return the mixture to a boil, and cook for 1 minute, stirring constantly. Remove from the heat.

Pour the filling into the sieve and press through with a spatula. Allow the filling to cool for about 5 minutes, stirring occasionally to prevent a skin from forming.

Add the butter 1 tablespoon at a time, whisking until each one is incorporated before adding the next. Pour into the prebaked pie shell and press a piece of plastic wrap directly on top of the filling. Refrigerate until firm, at least 3 hours.

Before serving, whip the heavy cream to soft peaks, add the confectioners' sugar and vanilla extract, and continue whipping just until the cream holds stiff peaks. Remove the plastic wrap from the pie and spread the whipped cream over the filling. Refrigerate until serving.

The pie will keep refrigerated for up to 2 days.

Derby Pie

This pie is named for the one and only Kentucky Derby. In the early days of the pie shop, we would take requests for special pies. A customer called and asked for "a mint-julep-esque pie" to take along on an RV trip from Brooklyn to the Derby. Mint and chocolate are a delicious combination, and adding a little bourbon never hurts anything.

Makes one 9-inch pie
Serves 8 to 10

All-Butter Crust for a 9-inch single-crust pie (see page 207), partially prebaked (see page 68)

1 cup whole milk

1 cup heavy cream

12 ounces bittersweet chocolate (55% cocoa), chopped into ¼-inch pieces

½ teaspoon kosher salt

2 large eggs

¼ teaspoon peppermint extract

2 to 3 tablespoons bourbon

Dash Old Fashion bitters

Cocoa powder for dusting (optional)

Garnish the top with fresh mint leaves for a classic look if you like, and most definitely add a dollop of freshly whipped cream.

Position a rack in the center of the oven and preheat the oven to 325°F. Place the prebaked pie shell on a rimmed baking sheet.

Combine the milk and cream in a heavy-bottomed saucepan and bring just to a boil. Place the chocolate pieces in a large bowl and pour the hot cream over the top. Let stand for 5 minutes, and then add salt and whisk steadily until all the chocolate is melted.

Crack the eggs into a separate bowl and whisk. Slowly stream a small amount of the chocolate mixture into the eggs, whisking as you pour. Continue until the egg mixture feels warm to the touch, and then mix it back into the chocolate mixture. Add the peppermint extract, bourbon to taste, and bitters and whisk until smooth.

Strain the filling through a fine-mesh sieve directly into the pie shell, or strain it into a separate bowl and then pour it into the shell. Bake on the middle rack of the oven for 30 to 35 minutes, rotating 180 degrees when the edges start to set, 20 to 25 minutes through baking. The pie is finished when the edges are set about 2 inches in and puffed slightly and the center is no longer liquid but still quite wobbly. Be careful not to overbake or the filling will be dry and sandy; the filling will continue to cook and set after the pie is removed from the oven. Allow to cool completely on a wire rack, 2 to 3 hours. If desired, dust with cocoa powder. Serve slightly warm or at room temperature.

The pie will keep refrigerated for 2 days or at room temperature for 1 day.

Pistachio Coconut Cream Pie

Makes one 9-inch pie
Serves 8 to 10

This recipe elevates the classic diner coconut cream pie with a richer, bolder flavor because of the pistachios in both the filling and the crust. This is a light, smooth, and creamy pie that is most definitely hard to stop eating.

Pistachio Coconut Crust (see page 213)

This recipe is *gluten-free!* Sprinkle toasted or untoasted coconut or crushed pistachios on top as a garnish.

²/₃ cup shelled pistachios, raw and unsalted
2½ cups whole milk
5 large egg yolks, whisked
6 tablespoons cornstarch
¾ cup granulated sugar
½ teaspoon kosher salt
1¼ cups coconut milk
2- to 3-inch strip lime zest
3 tablespoons unsalted butter, at room temperature
1 teaspoon fresh lime juice
1 cup heavy cream
1 tablespoon confectioners' sugar

Chop the pistachios in a food processor fitted with the blade attachment until chopped into medium to fine pieces. Add the chopped nuts to a heavy-bottomed saucepan along with the whole milk. Bring just to a boil over medium heat, remove the pan from the heat, and cover. Set aside to steep for 15 to 20 minutes.

Meanwhile, have the whisked egg yolks ready in a large bowl. In a large heavy-bottomed saucepan, whisk together the cornstarch, granulated sugar, and salt. Whisk in the coconut milk and add the strip of lime zest. Strain the pistachios from the milk, then add the milk to the saucepan and whisk until combined. Cook over medium-high heat, stirring constantly, until bubbling and thick, about 5 minutes. Once the mixture boils, cook for about 2 minutes longer. Remove from the heat.

Slowly and carefully stream one-third of the hot milk mixture into the yolks, whisking constantly to prevent the yolks from cooking. Stream in the remaining hot milk, and then return the mixture to the saucepan.

Have a large bowl ready for cooling and a fine-mesh sieve to strain the mixture through. Cook over medium heat, stirring constantly, until the mixture just returns to a boil, 1 to 2 minutes. Strain through the sieve, using a spatula to push the mixture through and to scrape the filling clinging to the bottom of the sieve. Allow to cool for 5 minutes, stirring occasionally to prevent a skin from forming.

Stir in the butter 1 tablespoon at a time, fully incorporating each addition before adding the next. Stir in the lime juice. Pour into the prepared crust and press a piece of plastic wrap directly onto the surface of the filling. Refrigerate until firm, about 4 hours.

In the chilled bowl of an electric mixer, beat the cream on medium speed until soft peaks form. Add the confectioners' sugar and continue beating on medium-low speed just until the cream holds stiff peaks. Remove the plastic wrap from the surface of the filling and spread the cream over the pie. Slice and serve.

The pie will keep refrigerated for 2 days.

Apple Rose Pie

Makes one 9-inch pie
Serves 8 to 10

While apples are not exactly in season in the spring, they are still readily available at farmers' markets through the magic of cold storage. We are able to source apples from our favorite farmers at Wilklow Orchards all year through. The addition of rose water is our homage to the springtime roses that line the sidewalks of Brooklyn in May.

This pie can also be made with a combination of apples and pears.

All-Butter Crust for a 9-inch double-crust pie (see page 207)

Juice of 2 lemons
6 to 7 baking apples (about 6 cups sliced)
1/3 cup plus 2 tablespoons granulated sugar
1/3 cup packed light brown sugar
2 tablespoons all-purpose flour
1/4 teaspoon ground allspice
1/4 teaspoon ground cinnamon
Pinch ground white pepper
1/2 teaspoon kosher salt
3 tablespoons rose water
Dash Angostura bitters
Egg wash (1 large egg whisked with 1 teaspoon water and a pinch of salt)
Demerara sugar, for finishing

Have ready and refrigerated one pastry-lined 9-inch pie pan and pastry round or lattice to top (see pages 56 and 58).

Pour the lemon juice into a large bowl. Prepare the apples using an apple-peeling machine, or core, peel, and thinly slice them with a sharp knife or on a mandoline. Dredge the apple slices in the lemon juice. Sprinkle with 2 tablespoons of the granulated sugar. Set aside to soften slightly and release some of the juices, 20 to 30 minutes.

In a large bowl, combine the remaining 1/3 cup granulated sugar, brown sugar, flour, allspice, cinnamon, white pepper, and salt. Drain any excess liquid from the apples, and toss with the sugar mixture. Sprinkle with the rose water and bitters.

Tightly layer the apples in the prepared pie shell so that there are minimal gaps, mounding the apples slightly higher in the center. Arrange the pastry round or lattice on top of the pie, and crimp the edges as desired (see pages 58 and 64).

Chill the pie in the refrigerator for 10 to 15 minutes to set the pastry. Meanwhile, position the oven racks in the bottom and center positions, place a rimmed baking sheet on the bottom rack, and preheat the oven to 425°F.

Brush the pastry with the egg wash to coat, and sprinkle with the desired amount of demerara sugar. Place the pie on the rimmed baking sheet on the lowest rack of the oven. Bake for 20 to 25 minutes, or until the pastry is set and beginning to brown. Lower the oven temperature to 375°F, move the pie to the center oven rack, and continue to bake until the pastry is a deep golden brown and the juices are bubbling, 30 to 35 minutes longer. Test the apples for doneness with a skewer or sharp knife; they should be tender and offer just the slightest resistance.

Allow to cool completely on a wire rack, 2 to 3 hours. Serve slightly warm or at room temperature.

The pie will keep refrigerated for 3 days or at room temperature for 2 days.

Lemon Verbena Raspberry Galette

About two doors down from the pie shop, we have a talented rooftop farmer and neighbor named Frieda Lim. She helped us build window boxes that overflow each summer with fresh herbs for our kitchen. Lemon verbena grows abundantly, and we love the bright, citrusy flavor it lends to fresh spring berries. It's an amazing and underused herb.

Makes one 9-inch galette
Serves 6 to 8

All-Butter Crust for a 9-inch single-crust pie (see page 207)

1 tablespoon chopped lemon verbena leaves

½ cup granulated sugar

¼ cup packed light brown sugar

3 tablespoons ground arrowroot

1 tablespoon fresh lemon juice

3 cups raspberries

Egg wash (1 large egg whisked with 1 teaspoon water and a pinch of salt), optional

Demerara sugar, for finishing

Have ready and refrigerated one pastry round about 13 inches in diameter. Position a rack in the middle of the oven and preheat the oven to 400°F.

In the bowl of a food processor fitted with the blade attachment, process the lemon verbena leaves, granulated and brown sugars, and arrowroot until the leaves are incorporated. Toss the sugar mixture and the lemon juice with the raspberries to coat. Assemble the galette (see page 67) on a rimmed baking sheet lined with parchment paper.

Brush the crust edge with egg wash if desired, and sprinkle all over with demerara sugar. Bake on the middle rack of the oven until the crust is golden brown and the filling is bubbling throughout, 35 to 40 minutes.

Allow to cool on a wire rack for at least 30 minutes. Serve warm or at room temperature.

The galette will keep refrigerated for 3 days or at room temperature for 2 days.

A galette is a free-form pastry that you bake directly on a baking sheet. Be creative with the way you shape and cut your galette; make sure to let it rest in the fridge until well chilled before baking to help it hold its shape. See the "Techniques" section for more details (page 67).

Rhuby Razz Square Pie

Makes one 8 x 8-inch
square
Serves 4 to 6

If you absolutely insist,
this recipe can be made
with strawberries instead
of raspberries, but
reduce the granulated
sugar by ¼ cup.

Though we claim to be rhubarb purists as our grandmother was, we do believe it pairs very well with tart raspberries.

All-Butter Crust for a 9-inch double-crust pie (see page 207)

About 1 pound fresh rhubarb, cut into ½-inch pieces (2½ cups)
2 cups raspberries
⅔ cup granulated sugar
⅔ cup packed light brown sugar
3 tablespoons ground arrowroot
½ teaspoon ground cinnamon
¼ teaspoon ground cardamom
½ teaspoon kosher salt
1 large egg
Dash Angostura bitters
Egg wash (1 large egg whisked with 1 teaspoon water and a pinch of salt)
Demerara sugar, for finishing

Roll the dough as directed on page 54 and fit into a well-greased 8 x 8 x 2-inch baking pan. Trim the excess, leaving about a ¾-inch overhang. Roll a lattice as directed on page 58. Refrigerate both for at least 30 minutes.

Combine the rhubarb, raspberries, granulated and brown sugars, arrowroot, cinnamon, cardamom, and salt in a large bowl and toss to combine. Stir in the egg and bitters. Pour the filling into the chilled pastry shell, arrange the lattice on top, and crimp as desired (see pages 58 and 64).

Chill the pie in the refrigerator for 10 to 15 minutes to set the pastry. Meanwhile, position the oven racks in the bottom and center positions, place a rimmed baking sheet on the bottom rack, and preheat the oven to 425°F.

Brush the pastry with the egg wash to coat, being careful not to drag the filling onto the pastry (it will burn). Sprinkle with the desired amount of demerara sugar.

Place the pie on the rimmed baking sheet on the lowest rack of the oven. Bake for 20 to 25 minutes, or until the pastry is set and beginning to brown. Lower the oven temperature to 375°F, move the pie to the center oven rack, and continue to bake until the pastry is a deep golden brown and the juices are bubbling throughout, 30 to 35 minutes longer.

Allow to cool completely on a wire rack, 2 to 3 hours. Serve slightly warm or at room temperature.

The pie will keep refrigerated for 3 days or at room temperature for 2 days.

Farmer Cheese with Thyme Pie

Farmer cheese is a soft, unripened cheese with a texture similar to ricotta's. This recipe is more savory than sweet but has a little sweetness from the honey along with the herbal notes of thyme. It is best served at brunch, as a savory appetizer or afternoon snack, or if you're feeling fancy, make it part of a cheese course for dessert.

Makes one 10-inch pie
Serves 8 to 10

All-Butter Crust for a 10-inch single-crust pie (see page 207), partially prebaked (see page 68)

2 cups farmer cheese
½ cup whole milk
⅓ cup honey
1 teaspoon fresh thyme
¼ teaspoon kosher salt
3 large eggs

If you can't find farmer cheese, a good, rich ricotta is a fine substitute.

Position a rack in the center of the oven and preheat the oven to 350°F. Place the prebaked pie shell on a rimmed baking sheet.

Combine the farmer cheese, milk, honey, thyme, and salt and stir well. Add the eggs one at a time and stir until well blended.

Pour the filling into the shell (it will be shallow) and bake on the middle rack of the oven for 35 to 40 minutes, rotating 180 degrees when the edges start to set, 25 to 30 minutes through baking. The pie is finished when the edges are set and puffed slightly and the center is no longer liquid but still quite wobbly. Be careful not to overbake or the filling will be dry; the filling will continue to cook and set after the pie is removed from the oven. Allow to cool completely on a wire rack, 2 to 3 hours. Serve at room temperature or cool.

The pie will keep refrigerated for 2 days or at room temperature for 1 day.

Sour Cherry Pie

Makes one 9-inch pie
Serves 8 to 10

The arrival of ripe sour cherries at the market is a sure sign that spring is in full bloom in New York and summer is just around the corner. Slightly smaller than a sweet cherry, the sour cherry boasts a truly incomparable flavor. While they are in season, we make as many sour cherry pies as we can.

All-Butter Crust for a 9-inch double-crust pie (see page 207)

5 cups sour cherries, pitted
1 tablespoon fresh lemon juice
¾ cup granulated sugar
¼ cup packed light brown sugar
3 tablespoons ground arrowroot
½ teaspoon ground allspice
½ teaspoon kosher salt
1 large egg
2 dashes Angostura bitters
Egg wash (1 large egg whisked with 1 teaspoon water and a pinch of salt)
Demerara sugar, for finishing

We like arrowroot as a thickening agent; it holds up to the acidity of the cherries without getting gummy as cornstarch easily can. Ground tapioca is a fair substitute if you can't find arrowroot; see the "Ingredients" section for more tips on starches.

Have ready and refrigerated one pastry-lined 9-inch pie pan and pastry round or lattice to top (see pages 56 and 58).

Combine the cherries, lemon juice, granulated and brown sugars, arrowroot, allspice, salt, egg, and bitters in a large bowl and toss well to combine. Pour the filling into the refrigerated pie shell, arrange the lattice or pastry round on top, and crimp as desired (see pages 58 and 64).

Chill the pie in the refrigerator for 10 to 15 minutes to set the pastry. Meanwhile, position the oven racks in the bottom and center positions, place a rimmed baking sheet on the bottom rack, and preheat the oven to 425°F.

Brush the pastry with the egg wash to coat; if your pie has a lattice top, be careful not to drag the filling onto the pastry (it will burn). Sprinkle with the desired amount of demerara sugar.

Place the pie on the rimmed baking sheet on the lowest rack of the oven. Bake for 20 to 25 minutes, or until the pastry is set and beginning to brown. Lower the oven temperature to 375°F, move the pie to the center oven rack, and continue to bake until the pastry is a deep golden brown and the juices are bubbling throughout, 30 to 35 minutes longer.

Allow to cool completely on a wire rack, 2 to 3 hours. Serve slightly warm or at room temperature.

The pie will keep refrigerated for 3 days or at room temperature for 2 days.

Summer

Summer

Summertime pies are all about the fruit. When the season really gets rolling, the pace at the shop is fast and furious. Our days and nights are filled with peeling, coring, hulling, slicing, and quartering a great variety of fruit grown in New York and New Jersey. Our favorite source for the majority of our summer fruits is Wilklow Orchards, a sixth-generation orchard and farm in the rolling hills of upstate New York's Hudson Valley. The Wilklow family, whom we first met when we were seeking a local source for rhubarb at the Brooklyn farmers' markets we frequent, has been working their land since 1855.

These days, the Wilklow family sell their fruit at the Brooklyn markets regularly. We were so excited to find a great local source for rhubarb. (Our father had been shipping it to us from his farm in South Dakota!) Little did we know that they would be able to provide us with an abundance of fruits, including strawberries, blackberries, raspberries, gooseberries, currants, sweet and sour cherries, peaches, nectarines, plums, pears, and, most important, apples. With the utilization of cold storage, they are able to provide us with delicious locally grown apples year-round. We truly believe it makes all the difference for our apple pies.

Sourcing fruit locally and in season will make your pies taste and look so much better than frozen or canned fruit will—not to mention, that's the way our grandmother did it. This is not to say that you can't freeze or jar your own fruit for use in pies—you will have good results as well. The "local, in-season" part is what's important. Fruit that has been picked unripe and shipped in a box across the country will never taste as good as fruit that's been ripened on the tree and brought into your kitchen that same day. A slice of pie made with freshly picked, sun-ripened fruit is like summer on a plate—enough said.

Sweet Cherry Streusel Pie

Makes one 9-inch pie
Serves 8 to 10

Cherry season at the pie shop is, well, the pits—that is, for those of us who have to prep a whole case of cherries at a time. For the cherry pie eaters of our community, never fear: whether it's a good year for cherries or a bad one, we aim to get our hands on as many cherries as possible. We spend hours pitting them (and eating our share) and making them into all manner of pies. One of our favorites is this streusel-topped beauty.

All-Butter Crust for a 9-inch single-crust pie (see page 207), partially prebaked (see page 68)

1⅔ cups streusel (see page 217), to top

1 small baking apple
5 cups sweet cherries, pitted
2 tablespoons fresh lemon juice
¾ cup packed light brown sugar
3 tablespoons potato starch
¼ teaspoon ground cinnamon
¼ teaspoon ground cardamom
2 dashes Angostura bitters

We are lucky enough to have our dedicated friends Rachel and Nutty, who come by the pie shop after hours to help pit cherries during fruit season. If you're planning to make more than one cherry pie, enlist your friends as pitter helpers! See the "Tools" section (see page 47) for tips on which cherry pitters we like best.

Have ready and refrigerated one partially prebaked pastry-lined 9-inch pie pan, crimped as desired (see page 64) and streusel to top. Position the oven racks in the bottom and center positions, place a rimmed baking sheet on the bottom rack, and preheat the oven to 425°F.

Peel the apple, and then shred it on the large holes of a box grater. Combine the shredded apple with the cherries, lemon juice, brown sugar, potato starch, cinnamon, cardamom, and bitters in a large bowl and toss until well mixed. Pour the filling into the refrigerated pie shell and evenly distribute the streusel on top.

Place the pie on the rimmed baking sheet on the lowest rack of the oven. Bake for 20 to 25 minutes, or until the pastry is set and beginning to brown. Lower the oven temperature to 375°F, move the pie to the center oven rack, and continue to bake until the pastry is a deep golden brown and the juices are bubbling throughout, 30 to 35 minutes longer.

Allow to cool completely on a wire rack, 2 to 3 hours. Serve slightly warm or at room temperature.

The pie will keep refrigerated for 3 days or at room temperature for 2 days.

Black & Blueberry Upside Down Pie

Growing up, we were lucky enough to eat some of the best pie within a hundred-mile radius, made by our grandma Liz. But on occasions when Mom wanted to take a break from the kitchen, we sometimes had little frozen chicken potpies, like those commercially made by Banquet, and we loved them. Our favorite thing to do was turn them out onto a plate and break them with a fork, allowing the steamy, hot filling to ooze out. This serving suggestion is in memory of that experience. Use a disposable aluminum pie tin, turn the pie out onto a large tray (we suggest 15 to 20 inches in diameter), put a few scoops of ice cream on top while it's still warm, and set it in the middle of the table for sharing. It's a pie party.

Makes one 9-inch pie
Serves 8 to 10

All-Butter Crust for a 9-inch double-crust pie (see page 207)

1 small baking apple
2 to 3 cups blackberries
2 to 3 cups blueberries
2 tablespoons fresh lemon juice
½ cup granulated sugar
¼ cup packed light brown sugar (or more if the berries are tart)
3 tablespoons ground arrowroot
½ teaspoon ground cinnamon
¼ teaspoon ground cardamom
Pinch ground cloves
½ teaspoon kosher salt
2 dashes Angostura bitters
Egg wash (1 large egg whisked with 1 teaspoon water and a pinch of salt)
Demerara sugar, for finishing

Turning this lovely pie on its head is merely a serving suggestion; it most definitely can be cooled, sliced, and served the same as any other pie (but may be a little less fun).

Have ready and refrigerated one pastry-lined 9-inch pie pan and pastry round or lattice to top (see pages 56 and 58).

Peel and then shred the apple on the large holes of a box grater. Combine with the blackberries, blueberries, lemon juice, granulated and brown sugars, arrowroot, cinnamon, cardamom, cloves, salt, and bitters in a large bowl and stir until well mixed. Pour the filling into the refrigerated pie shell, arrange the lattice or pastry round on top, and crimp as desired (see pages 58 and 64).

Chill the pie in the refrigerator for 10 to 15 minutes to set the pastry. Meanwhile, position the oven racks in the bottom and center positions, place a rimmed baking sheet on the bottom rack, and preheat the oven to 425°F.

(recipe continues)

Brush the pastry with the egg wash to coat; if your pie has a lattice top, be careful not to drag the filling onto the pastry (it will burn). Sprinkle with the desired amount of demerara sugar.

Place the pie on the rimmed baking sheet on the lowest rack of the oven. Bake for 20 to 25 minutes, or until the pastry is set and beginning to brown. Lower the oven temperature to 375°F, move the pie to the center oven rack, and continue to bake until the pastry is a deep golden brown and the juices are bubbling throughout, 30 to 35 minutes longer.

Allow to cool completely on a wire rack, 2 to 3 hours. Serve slightly warm or at room temperature.

The pie will keep refrigerated for 3 days or at room temperature for 2 days.

Bluebarb Slab Pie

Slab pies are the perfect way to feed pie to a crowd, and they are *the* pie for crust lovers—the crust-to-filling ratio is more evenly balanced, a perfect vehicle for any variety of summer fruits.

Makes one 16 x 12-inch slab pie
Serves 12 to 16

2 All-Butter Crusts for a 9-inch double-crust pie (see page 207)

1½ to 2 pounds fresh rhubarb, cut into ½-inch pieces (4 to 5 cups)
4 to 5 cups blueberries (about 1½ pounds fresh)
1 large baking apple (such as Northern Spy or Golden Delicious)
1 cup packed light brown sugar
⅔ cup granulated sugar (or more, depending on the tartness of the blueberries)
½ teaspoon ground allspice
½ teaspoon ground cinnamon
½ teaspoon ground cardamom
⅛ teaspoon ground cloves
¾ teaspoon kosher salt
7 tablespoons ground arrowroot
2 tablespoons fresh lemon juice
2 to 3 dashes cocktail bitters
Egg wash (1 large egg whisked with 1 teaspoon water and a pinch of salt)
Demerara sugar, for finishing

You can get creative with the way you decorate the top crust: a lattice, cutout shapes, or simple knife slits all work well.

Prepare the pie dough as directed on page 207, making each recipe into a single rectangle instead of two discs. Wrap in plastic and let chill as directed.

Butter the baking sheet well and line with parchment paper. On a lightly floured work surface, roll the dough into a 20 x 16-inch rectangle, or 3 to 4 inches larger than your baking sheet (we use a 16 x 11½ x 1-inch rimmed baking sheet). Fit the dough inside the sheet. Roll the second crust rectangle to a 17 x 13-inch rectangle. Lay in the pan on top of the bottom crust, folding in half if necessary, and place in the refrigerator to chill while you prepare the filling.

Combine the rhubarb and blueberries in a large bowl, crushing about half the blueberries with your hands as you add them. Peel the apple, shred on the large holes of a box grater, and add to the blueberries and rhubarb, along with the brown and granulated sugars, allspice, cinnamon, cardamom, cloves, salt, arrowroot, lemon juice, and cocktail bitters; mix thoroughly. Remove the prepared crusts from the fridge and set the top crust rectangle aside. Pour the filling into the pastry-lined baking sheet. Position the top crust rectangle squarely over the filling, and then roll and pinch the excess crust inward to create an edge all the way around the pan. Crimp this edge as desired. Create steam vents using a sharp paring knife.

(recipe continues)

Chill the pie in the refrigerator for 10 to 15 minutes to set the pastry. Meanwhile, position the oven racks in the bottom and center positions, place a rimmed baking sheet on the bottom rack, and preheat the oven to 425°F.

Brush the pastry with the egg wash and sprinkle with the desired amount of demerara sugar. Place the pie on the lowest oven rack and bake for 20 to 25 minutes, or until the pastry is set and beginning to brown. Lower the oven temperature to 375°F, move the pie to the center oven rack, and continue to bake until the pastry is a deep golden brown and the juices are bubbling throughout, 30 to 35 minutes longer.

Allow to cool completely on a wire rack, 2 to 3 hours. Serve slightly warm or at room temperature.

The pie will keep refrigerated for 3 days or at room temperature for 2 days.

Lavender Blueberry Pie

When picked at their peak, sun-ripened blueberries have a floral quality that pairs perfectly with lavender. Use a tiny bit of edible lavender oil for a subtle floral note.

Makes one 9-inch pie
Serves 8 to 10

All-Butter Crust for a 9-inch double-crust pie (see page 207)

1 small baking apple
5 to 6 cups blueberries (about 2 pounds fresh)
2 tablespoons fresh lemon juice
½ cup granulated sugar
¼ cup packed light brown sugar
3 tablespoons ground arrowroot
½ teaspoon ground allspice
½ teaspoon kosher salt
2 to 3 small drops food-grade lavender oil (see page 41 for source)
2 dashes Angostura bitters
Egg wash (1 large egg whisked with 1 teaspoon water and a pinch of salt)
Demerara sugar, for finishing

You can try to make your own lavender essence from fresh lavender as we did, but we found that the flavor comes through more reliably and easily when using edible lavender oil. (See our "Sourcing" section for suppliers.)

Have ready and refrigerated one pastry-lined 9-inch pie pan and pastry round or lattice to top (see pages 56 and 58).

Peel and then shred the apple on the large holes of a box grater. Combine with the blueberries, lemon juice, granulated and brown sugars, arrowroot, allspice, salt, lavender oil, and bitters in a large bowl and stir until well mixed, crushing some of the blueberries in the process (your hands work great for this). Pour the filling into the refrigerated pie shell, arrange the lattice or pastry round on top, and crimp as desired (see pages 58 and 64).

Chill the pie in the refrigerator for 10 to 15 minutes to set the pastry. Meanwhile, position the oven racks in the bottom and center positions, place a rimmed baking sheet on the bottom rack, and preheat the oven to 425°F.

Brush the pastry with the egg wash to coat; if your pie has a lattice top, be careful not to drag the filling onto the pastry (it will burn). Sprinkle with the desired amount of demerara sugar.

Place the pie on the rimmed baking sheet on the lowest rack of the oven. Bake for 20 to 25 minutes, or until the pastry is set and beginning to brown. Lower the oven temperature to 375°F, move the pie to the center oven rack, and continue to bake until the pastry is a deep golden brown and the juices are bubbling throughout, 30 to 35 minutes longer.

Cool completely on a wire rack, 2 to 3 hours. Serve warm or at room temperature. The pie will keep refrigerated for 3 days or at room temperature for 2 days.

Nectarine Blueberry Pie

Nectarines are an excellent pie fruit. They are easy to prep (no peeling required), they have a delicious, unique flavor, and when you mix them with blueberries, the resulting color is an elegant reddish purple with a flavor to match.

Makes one 9-inch pie
Serves 8 to 10

All-Butter Crust for a 9-inch double-crust pie (see page 207)

1 pound nectarines, sliced (3 cups)
2 to 3 cups blueberries
Pinch finely grated lemon zest
2 tablespoons fresh lemon juice
½ teaspoon ground allspice
Pinch ground cloves
½ teaspoon kosher salt
Dash Angostura bitters
Egg wash (1 large egg whisked with 1 teaspoon water and a pinch of salt)
Demerara sugar, for finishing

If blueberries are not available, raspberries, blackberries, or strawberries are excellent paired with nectarines as well.

Have ready and refrigerated one pastry-lined 9-inch pie pan and pastry round or lattice to top (see pages 56 and 58).

Combine the fruit, lemon zest and juice, allspice, cloves, salt, and bitters in a large bowl and stir well. Pour the filling into the refrigerated pie shell, arrange the lattice or pastry round on top, and crimp as desired (see pages 58 and 64).

Chill the pie in the refrigerator for 10 to 15 minutes to set the pastry. Meanwhile, position the oven racks in the bottom and center positions, place a rimmed baking sheet on the bottom rack, and preheat the oven to 425°F.

Brush the pastry with the egg wash to coat; if your pie has a lattice top, be careful not to drag the filling onto the pastry (it will burn). Sprinkle with the desired amount of demerara sugar.

Place the pie on the rimmed baking sheet on the lowest rack of the oven. Bake for 20 to 25 minutes, or until the pastry is set and beginning to brown. Lower the oven temperature to 375°F, move the pie to the center oven rack, and continue to bake until the pastry is a deep golden brown and the juices are bubbling throughout, 30 to 35 minutes longer.

Allow to cool completely on a wire rack, 2 to 3 hours. Serve slightly warm or at room temperature.

The pie will keep refrigerated for 3 days or at room temperature for 2 days.

Paprika Peach Pie

Makes one 9-inch pie
Serves 8 to 10

Paprika is typically used in savory dishes, but we were inspired to combine it with peaches after a close friend of the pie shop, Jill Mercedes, shared her unforgettable specialty dessert with us one evening after a long day of baking. Claiming to "not be a baker" (after one bite of her recipe, we had to disagree), Jill presented us with a rustic tart, with still warm oven-roasted peaches and a bit of cornmeal, and most important, finished with a sprinkling of paprika. The spice adds a sweet warmth to the peaches and enhances their lovely golden color.

All-Butter Crust for a 9-inch double-crust pie (see page 207)

There are a variety of paprikas on the market: spicy or mild, sweet or smoky. We tested quite a few for this recipe and found that a good sweet paprika pairs the best, but feel free to try out different varieties.

2½ pounds peaches (enough for about 5 cups sliced)
2 tablespoons fresh lemon juice
⅔ cup granulated sugar
¼ cup packed light brown sugar
3 tablespoons potato starch
1 tablespoon sweet paprika
⅛ teaspoon white pepper
¼ teaspoon allspice
¼ teaspoon ginger
½ teaspoon kosher salt
1 to 2 dashes Old Fashion bitters
Egg wash (1 large egg whisked with 1 teaspoon water and a pinch of salt)
Demerara sugar, for finishing

Have ready and refrigerated one pastry-lined 9-inch pie pan and pastry round or lattice to top (see pages 56 and 58).

Bring a large pot of water to a simmer. Have ready a large bowl of ice water. Score an X into the bottom of each peach, and then drop it into the simmering water for 30 to 60 seconds. Remove and immediately drop into the ice water. When the fruit has cooled slightly, the skin should slip off easily when scraped with the back of a knife.

Slice the peeled peaches into ½-inch slices, add to a large bowl, and sprinkle with the lemon juice. Add the granulated and brown sugars, potato starch, paprika, white pepper, allspice, ginger, salt, and bitters and toss well to combine. Spoon the filling into the refrigerated pie shell, leaving behind excess juices. Arrange the lattice or pastry round on top, and crimp as desired (see pages 58 and 64).

Chill the pie in the refrigerator for 10 to 15 minutes to set the pastry. Meanwhile, position the oven racks in the bottom and center positions, place a rimmed baking sheet on the bottom rack, and preheat the oven to 425°F.

Brush the pastry with the egg wash to coat; if your pie has a lattice top, be careful not to drag the filling onto the pastry (it will burn). Sprinkle with the desired amount of demerara sugar.

Place the pie on the rimmed baking sheet on the lowest rack of the oven. Bake for 20 to 25 minutes, or until the pastry is set and beginning to brown. Lower the oven temperature to 375°F, move the pie to the center oven rack, and continue to bake until the pastry is a deep golden brown and the juices are bubbling throughout, 30 to 35 minutes longer.

Allow to cool completely on a wire rack, 2 to 3 hours. Serve slightly warm or at room temperature.

The pie will keep refrigerated for 3 days or at room temperature for 2 days.

Peaches & Cream Pie

Makes one 9-inch pie
Serves 8 to 10

The crust for this peach pie is made from our crumble topping recipe—just press it into the pan as you would any crumb crust. The cream is a combination of cream cheese, sour cream, and spices. Use perfectly ripe peaches for the best result.

Oat Crumble Crust for a 9-inch pie, prebaked (see page 216)

1 pound fresh peaches (enough for 2 cups sliced)
2 tablespoons fresh lemon juice
2 tablespoons granulated sugar
½ cup packed light brown sugar
¼ cup cream cheese, softened
½ cup sour cream
¼ teaspoon ground allspice
¼ teaspoon kosher salt
1 large egg

This recipe is equally delicious with any ripe summer fruit: plums, nectarines, or berries are great choices.

Position a rack in the center of the oven and preheat the oven to 325°F. Place the prebaked pie shell on a rimmed baking sheet.

Bring a large pot of water to a simmer. Have ready a large bowl of ice water. Score an X into the bottom of each peach, and then drop it into the simmering water for 30 to 60 seconds. Remove and immediately drop into the ice water. When the fruit has cooled slightly, the skin should slip off easily when scraped with the back of a knife.

Slice the peeled peaches into 1-inch slices, add to a large bowl, and sprinkle with the lemon juice and granulated sugar.

In a medium bowl combine the brown sugar and cream cheese and blend until smooth. Mix in the sour cream, allspice, and salt, and then stir in the egg.

Pour a thin layer of the custard into the prepared oat crust. Starting from the center, arrange the peach slices in a spiral pattern. Pour the remaining custard over the top.

Bake on the middle rack of the oven for 35 to 40 minutes, rotating 180 degrees when the edges start to set, about 25 minutes through baking. The pie is finished when the outer 2 inches are set but the center still wobbles slightly. Be careful not to overbake or the custard can separate; the filling will continue to cook and set after the pie is removed from the oven. Allow to cool completely on a wire rack, about 1 hour. Serve at room temperature or cool.

The pie will keep refrigerated for 2 days or at room temperature for 1 day.

Plumble Pie

This recipe for pie in a bowl is dedicated to all fans of pie for breakfast. Add a scoop of fresh tangy yogurt and you've got a hearty bowl of crumble-topped goodness to start the day. You can substitute other stone fruits for the plums if you wish: peaches, nectarines, and apricots work well. Use sturdy oven-safe bowls and bake on a baking sheet.

Makes four 4-inch or two 6-inch bowls
Serves 4 to 8

All-Butter Crust for a 9-inch single-crust pie (see page 207)

2 cups Oat Crumble (see page 216), to top

2 pounds plums, sliced (4 to 5 cups)
2 tablespoons fresh lemon juice
½ cup granulated sugar
½ cup packed light brown sugar
3 tablespoons potato starch
¼ teaspoon ground allspice
¼ teaspoon ground ginger
¼ teaspoon ground cardamom
2 dashes Old Fashion bitters

If you'd like this pie to be more tart than sweet, it's fine to reduce the sugar, especially if your plums are nice and ripe.

Divide the dough into 2 or 4 pieces, depending on the size of bowls being used. Roll each piece into a disc 2 to 3 inches larger than the bowl (see page 54 for rolling instructions). Grease the bowls well and fit the dough inside; crimp the edges as desired (see page 64). Refrigerate for at least 30 minutes.

Position the oven racks in the bottom and center positions, place a rimmed baking sheet on the bottom rack, and preheat the oven to 425°F.

Combine the plums, lemon juice, granulated and brown sugars, potato starch, allspice, ginger, cardamom, and bitters in a large bowl and mix well.

Place the bowls on the rimmed baking sheet and distribute the plum filling evenly among them. Top with the oat crumble. Bake on the lowest rack of the oven for 20 to 25 minutes, or until the pastry is set and beginning to brown. Lower the oven temperature to 375°F, move the pies to the center oven rack, and continue to bake until the pastry is a deep golden brown and the juices are bubbling throughout, 30 to 35 minutes longer.

Allow the bowls to cool completely on a wire rack, 1 to 2 hours. Serve slightly warm or at room temperature.

The pie will keep refrigerated for 3 days or at room temperature for 2 days.

White Nectarine & Red Currant Pie

Makes one 10-inch pie
in a tart pan
Serves 8 to 10

Currants are a beautiful and dainty berry that appear early in the summer. Their tart and seedy character pairs well with stone fruits—whose sweetness helps offset the sour bite of berries—and their color creates a delicate pink shade.

All-Butter Crust for a 10-inch double-crust pie (see page 207)

You can try black or
champagne currants
with this recipe as well.

1½ pounds fresh white nectarines, sliced (4 cups)
1 cup fresh red currants
2 tablespoons fresh lemon juice
3 tablespoons potato starch
½ teaspoon cinnamon
½ teaspoon kosher salt
Dash Old Fashion bitters
Egg wash (1 large egg whisked with 1 teaspoon water and a pinch of salt)
Demerara sugar, for finishing

Have ready and refrigerated one pastry-lined 10-inch tart pan (see page 57) and a 12-inch pastry round to top. Position the oven racks in the bottom and center positions and preheat the oven to 425°F.

Combine the fruits, lemon juice, potato starch, cinnamon, salt, and bitters in a large bowl and mix well. Place the pastry-lined tart pan on a rimmed baking sheet and pour in the filling. Center and lay the top pastry round over the filling. Press the pastry edges together to seal, and trim off any excess pastry. If desired, create a decorative crosshatching effect on the top by lightly scoring lines from one side to the other with a sharp knife. Brush with the egg wash and sprinkle with the desired amount of demerara sugar.

Place on the lowest rack of the oven and bake for 20 to 25 minutes, or until the pastry is set and beginning to brown. Lower the oven temperature to 375°F, move the pie to the center oven rack, and continue to bake until the pastry is a deep golden brown and the juices are bubbling throughout, 30 to 35 minutes longer.

Allow to cool completely on a wire rack, 2 to 3 hours. Serve slightly warm or at room temperature.

The pie will keep refrigerated for 3 days or at room temperature for 2 days.

Black Currant Lemon Chiffon Pie

Makes one 9-inch pie
Serves 8 to 10

Often in the heat of summer, turning on the oven for more than an hour to bake a pie is the last thing you want to do. Prebaking the crust for this recipe is optional. This is the perfect pie for making at the lake or beach house—the crumb crust is made from store-bought animal crackers, and the chiffon filling is set with gelatin. If you put this pie together in the morning, it will easily be ready by grilling time.

Animal Cracker Crumb Crust for a 9-inch pie (see page 209), prebaked or refrigerated until firm

This recipe is tart and citrusy, so if you prefer a sweeter pie, add an additional ¼ cup of confectioners' sugar to the heavy cream when whipping. If you can't get your hands on black currants, try blueberries or blackberries, and adjust the sugar according to taste and the ripeness of the berries.

1½ cups black currants

1½ cups granulated sugar

1½ tablespoons ground arrowroot

2 tablespoons water

½ teaspoon kosher salt

1 package unflavored gelatin

¼ cup fresh orange juice

1 teaspoon finely grated orange zest

1 teaspoon finely grated lemon zest

½ cup fresh lemon juice (from 3 to 4 lemons)

4 large egg yolks

2 large egg whites

½ teaspoon vanilla extract

½ cup confectioners' sugar

¾ cup heavy cream

Combine the black currants, 1 cup of the granulated sugar, the arrowroot, the water, and ¼ teaspoon of the kosher salt in a heavy-bottomed saucepan; bring to a simmer over medium heat and continue to cook until reduced by half, 12 to 15 minutes. Position a fine-mesh sieve on the rim of a bowl; pour in the black currant sauce and press through with the back of a spatula. Pour the sauce (you should have about ½ cup) into the crumb crust and carefully spread in an even layer. Refrigerate until ready to fill.

Sprinkle the gelatin evenly over the orange juice in a medium bowl to soften. In a medium metal bowl, combine the orange and lemon zests, lemon juice, remaining ½ cup granulated sugar, egg yolks, and remaining ¼ teaspoon salt. Place the bowl over a larger pot of simmering water, being sure to not let the bowl touch the water, and cook, stirring constantly, until the mixture is thickened to a custard-like consistency, 4 to 5 minutes. Remove from the heat and add the softened gelatin and vanilla; stir until dissolved. Refrigerate, stirring often, until the mixture thickens to a soft set, about 25 minutes. If the mixture thickens too much and becomes lumpy, soften it slightly by setting the bowl in a warm water bath and whisking just until smooth.

Beat the egg whites until fluffy, add the confectioners' sugar, and continue to beat until stiff peaks form. Set aside. In a separate bowl, beat the heavy cream until stiff but not grainy. Gently fold the lemon mixture into the beaten egg white in four additions. Follow in the same fashion by adding the whipped cream to the lemon–egg white mixture, folding until no clumps of cream or egg white remain, but taking care not to overmix or deflate the filling. Spoon the mixture over the black currant sauce in the prepared shell and refrigerate until firm, at least 3 hours.

Serve cold; remove the pie from the refrigerator 20 minutes before slicing to make serving easier.

The pie will keep refrigerated for 2 days.

Black Currant Bitties

Black currants are still somewhat rare in the United States because of a longtime ban (now lifted) on their growth—they can carry a fungus that kills evergreen trees; who knew? Lucky for us, our favorite growers, Wilklow Orchards, has a small crop each year, and we are always excited to get them. This recipe highlights their unique flavor.

Makes 24 bite-size pies

All-Butter Crust for a 9-inch single-crust pie (see page 207)

1 small (or ½ large) baking apple
1 cup fresh black currants
½ cup packed light brown sugar
¼ cup granulated sugar
1 large egg
1 tablespoon ground arrowroot
⅛ teaspoon ground allspice
⅛ teaspoon ground cinnamon
⅛ teaspoon kosher salt
Pinch finely grated lemon or orange zest
Confectioners' sugar, to finish

Any berry will work for this recipe; adjust the sugar according to taste and the ripeness of your berries.

Separate the dough into 24 equal pieces (the easiest way is to divide the dough in half, and then continue dividing each piece into halves until you have 24). Roll each piece into a ball and place in the cup of a well-greased mini-muffin pan. Use the back of a rounded teaspoon to push down into the center of the dough ball so it lines the cup. Use your fingers to finish pushing the dough into place; the crust rim should come above the level of the pan. Make sure the bottom isn't too thick. Freeze until solid.

Position a rack in the lower third of the oven and preheat the oven to 400°F. Peel the apple and then shred it on the small holes of a box grater. Stir it together with the black currants, brown and granulated sugars, egg, arrowroot, allspice, cinnamon, salt, and zest in a medium bowl. Place the muffin tin on a rimmed baking sheet and portion 1 tablespoon of filling into each of the frozen pastry cups. Place in the lower third of the oven and bake until the crust is golden brown and the filling is bubbling, about 30 minutes.

Allow to cool completely on a wire rack, about 1 hour. Serve slightly warm or at room temperature. Dust with confectioners' sugar just before serving.

The pies will keep refrigerated for 3 days or at room temperature for 2 days.

Skillet Stone Fruit Streusel Pie

Makes one 8- or 9-inch
skillet pie
Serves 6 to 8

Stone fruits include any fruit in which the fleshy edible part surrounds a hard shell with a seed inside. Plums, peaches, nectarines, apricots, and cherries are all considered stone fruits. For this recipe, you can use any combination of stone fruit that you can get your hands on, or any pairing that sounds tasty to you. Just be sure to adjust the brown sugar, to taste, accordingly.

Cornmeal Crust for a 9-inch single-crust pie (see page 211)

1⅔ cups streusel (see page 217), to top

To make this pie in a
larger skillet, just double
the recipe; you may have
a little extra filling and
crust, which you could
shape into a little galette.

4 cups mixed stone fruit, whole, halved, or quartered, pits removed
2 tablespoons fresh lemon juice
¾ cup packed light brown sugar
¼ teaspoon ground cinnamon
¼ teaspoon ground ginger
Pinch cloves
½ teaspoon kosher salt
Dash Angostura bitters

Roll out the crust as instructed on page 54. Fit into a greased 8- or 9-inch skillet and trim the overhang to 1½ inches. Refrigerate for at least 30 minutes.

Position the oven racks in the bottom and center positions, place a rimmed baking sheet on the bottom rack, and preheat the oven to 425°F.

Combine the stone fruit, lemon juice, brown sugar to taste, cinnamon, ginger, cloves, salt, and bitters in a large bowl and mix well.

Place the skillet on the rimmed baking sheet and pour in the filling. Fold in the overhang to lie on top of the fruit; top with the streusel. Bake on the lowest rack of the oven for 20 to 25 minutes, or until the pastry is set and beginning to brown. Lower the oven temperature to 375°F, move the pie to the center oven rack, and continue to bake until the pastry is a deep golden brown and the juices are bubbling throughout, 30 to 35 minutes longer.

Allow to cool completely on a wire rack, 2 to 3 hours. Serve slightly warm or at room temperature.

The pie will keep refrigerated for 3 days or at room temperature for 2 days.

Apple Blackberry Rounds

Makes 8 rounds

Freshly picked, sun-ripened blackberries are worth their weight in gold. They have a tart and sweet perfume that far surpasses that of store-bought varieties. When you see them at your local farmers' market, take home a couple of pints and make these sweet little rounds, which are a twist on an all-time classic pie. Use a hand-cranked peeler for the apples and a round biscuit cutter for the crust to make it easy to assemble these little pastries.

All-Butter Crust for a 9-inch double-crust pie (see page 207)

These kid-size pies are a great project to work on with the little ones; they fit perfectly into lunch boxes (and pockets).

3 to 4 medium baking apples
2 tablespoons fresh lemon juice
½ cup granulated sugar
1 cup fresh blackberries
¼ cup packed light brown sugar
1½ tablespoons all-purpose flour
⅛ teaspoon cinnamon
⅛ teaspoon allspice
Pinch freshly ground black pepper
Egg wash (1 large egg whisked with 1 teaspoon water and a pinch of salt)
Demerara sugar, for finishing

Roll the dough into two circles as directed on page 54. Use a 3-inch and a 4-inch biscuit cutter to cut four circles of each size from each of the dough discs for a total of 16 discs. Lay the circles on a baking sheet lined with parchment paper and refrigerate while you prepare the filling.

Prepare the apples using an apple-peeling machine, or core, peel, and thinly slice them crosswise with a sharp knife or on a mandoline to ¼ inch or less. Sprinkle the apple slices with the lemon juice and 2 tablespoons of the granulated sugar. Set aside to soften slightly and release some of the juices, 20 to 30 minutes.

In a small bowl, toss the blackberries with 2 tablespoons of the granulated sugar. Whisk together the remaining ¼ cup granulated sugar, brown sugar, flour, cinnamon, allspice, and black pepper. Drain the apples of excess liquid and toss with the sugar mixture to coat.

To assemble, place the 3-inch rounds on a baking sheet lined with parchment paper and brush the outer 1-inch circle with egg wash or water. Stack 2 to 3 apple slices on each round and place 1 or 2 blackberries in the center hole. Position the 4-inch crust circle over the apples and press the top and bottom crust edges together with the tines of a fork. Chill the rounds in the refrigerator for 10 to 15 minutes to set the pastry. Meanwhile, position an oven rack in the center position and preheat the oven to 400°F.

Brush the rounds with the egg wash to coat, cut an X-shaped steam vent in the center, and sprinkle with the desired amount of demerara sugar. Place the baking sheet on the center rack of the oven and bake until the pastry is golden brown and the apples are tender when tested with a skewer or sharp knife, about 30 minutes.

Allow to cool on a wire rack for about 20 minutes. Serve warm or at room temperature.

The rounds will keep refrigerated for 3 days or at room temperature for 2 days.

Cinnamon Apricot Pie with Vanilla Pouring Cream

Makes one 9-inch pie
Serves 8 to 10

The combination of cinnamon and apricot is quite simply warm and comforting, making this the perfect late summer dessert when cooler nights are in the forecast.

All-Butter Crust for a 9-inch double-crust pie (see page 207)

Cinnamon is the star of this recipe; be sure to use a quality one. See the "Sourcing" section for online spice merchants we recommend.

2 tablespoons fresh lemon juice

1½ pounds apricots, quartered and stones removed (4 to 5 cups)

¾ cup granulated sugar

¼ cup packed light brown sugar

1 teaspoon ground cinnamon

½ teaspoon kosher salt

3 tablespoons potato starch

3 dashes Angostura or Old Fashion bitters

Egg wash (1 large egg whisked with 1 teaspoon water and a pinch of salt)

Demerara sugar, for finishing

Vanilla Pouring Cream, to serve (recipe follows)

Have ready and refrigerated one pastry-lined 9-inch pie pan and pastry round or lattice to top (see pages 56 and 58).

Sprinkle the lemon juice over the prepared apricots to prevent browning. In a separate bowl, whisk together the granulated and brown sugars, cinnamon, salt, and potato starch. Toss the sugar mixture with the apricots and bitters.

Pour the filling into the refrigerated pie shell, arrange the lattice or pastry round on top, and crimp as desired (see pages 58 and 64). Chill the pie in the refrigerator for 10 to 15 minutes to set the pastry. Meanwhile, position the oven racks in the bottom and center positions, place a rimmed baking sheet on the bottom rack, and preheat the oven to 425°F.

Brush the pastry with the egg wash to coat; if your pie has a lattice top, be careful not to drag the filling onto the pastry (it will burn). Sprinkle with the desired amount of demerara sugar.

Place the pie on the rimmed baking sheet on the lowest rack of the oven. Bake for 20 to 25 minutes, or until the pastry is set and beginning to brown. Lower the oven temperature to 375°F, move the pie to the center oven rack, and continue to bake until the pastry is a deep golden brown and the juices are bubbling throughout, 30 to 35 minutes longer.

Allow to cool completely on a wire rack, 2 to 3 hours. Serve slightly warm or at room temperature. The pie will keep refrigerated for 3 days or at room temperature for 2 days.

Vanilla Pouring Cream

2 cups whole milk

4 large egg yolks

1 teaspoon cornstarch

4 tablespoons granulated sugar

1 teaspoon vanilla paste (Nielsen-Massey makes a readily available one)

1 to 2 tablespoons dark rum (optional)

Position a fine-mesh sieve on the rim of a medium bowl.

In a heavy-bottomed saucepan over medium heat, bring the milk just to a boil. Meanwhile, whisk together the yolks, cornstarch, and sugar until thick and light colored. Slowly stream about half the hot milk mixture into the yolk mixture, whisking constantly. Add the hot yolk mixture back to the saucepan and cook over low heat until the mixture is thick enough to coat the back of a spoon.

Strain the custard through the sieve, and then stir in the vanilla paste and dark rum (if using). Serve warm.

The custard will keep refrigerated for up to 3 days.

Muskmelon Chiffon Pie

Salting melon is a matter of taste, but the salt actually brings out the sweetness of a good ripe melon. That simple combination of salt and melon was our inspiration for this light, summery pie paired with a saltine cracker crust. The approach is a relatively traditional chiffon, using gelatin and egg yolk and whipped egg whites for a firm, smooth filling. You will need an electric juicer to juice the melon. Try different heirloom melon varieties with this if you can find them.

Makes one 9-inch pie
Serves 8 to 10

Saltine Crust for a 9-inch pie (see page 215), prebaked or refrigerated until firm

1½ envelopes (4 teaspoons) unflavored gelatin

2 cups fresh melon juice (from about ½ large cantaloupe)

3 large egg yolks

⅓ cup granulated sugar

⅛ teaspoon ground anise

¼ teaspoon kosher salt

1 tablespoon fresh lime juice

10 lemon balm leaves, torn

2 large egg whites

2 tablespoons confectioners' sugar

½ cup heavy cream

If you don't have lemon balm, you can use regular fresh mint. Don't be afraid to combine this awesome saltine crust with other pies in this book. Prebaking the crust is optional if you don't want to turn the oven on.

In a large bowl, sprinkle the gelatin evenly over ¼ cup of the melon juice. In a medium metal bowl, whisk together the remaining 1¾ cups melon juice, egg yolks, granulated sugar, anise, salt, lime juice, and lemon balm leaves. Place the bowl over a larger pot of simmering water, being sure the bowl does not touch the water, and cook, stirring constantly, until the mixture is thickened to a custard-like consistency, about 8 minutes. Remove from the heat and add the softened gelatin; stir until dissolved. Refrigerate, stirring often, until the mixture thickens to a soft set, 25 to 30 minutes.

Beat the egg whites until fluffy, add the confectioners' sugar, and continue to beat until stiff peaks form. Set aside. In a separate bowl, beat the heavy cream until stiff but not grainy. Gently fold the melon mixture into the beaten egg white in four additions. Follow in the same fashion by adding the melon–egg white mixture to the whipped cream, folding until no clumps of cream or egg white remain, but taking care not to overmix or deflate the filling. Spoon the mixture into the prepared shell and refrigerate until firm, at least 3 hours. Serve cold; remove from the refrigerator 20 minutes before slicing to make serving easier.

The pie will keep refrigerated for 2 days.

Gooseberry Galette

Makes one 9-inch galette
Serves 6 to 8

Gooseberries are furry berries that grow on dangerously spiky branches. They are somewhat hard to come by and have a unique flavor that is only enhanced when baked. Making them into a galette is the perfect treatment, especially if you can get your hands on only a pint or two.

All-Butter Crust for a 9-inch single-crust pie (see page 207)

3 cups gooseberries, stems removed

1 cup granulated sugar

3 tablespoons ground arrowroot

Pinch finely grated lemon zest

1 tablespoon fresh lemon juice

¼ teaspoon allspice

¼ teaspoon kosher salt

Egg wash (1 large egg whisked with 1 teaspoon water and a pinch of salt), optional

Demerara sugar, for finishing

If you happen to have a lot of gooseberries on hand, you can double this recipe to make enough filling for a double-crusted pie. But adjust sugar according to taste and tartness of the berries.

Have ready and refrigerated one pastry round about 13 inches in diameter. Line a rimmed baking sheet with parchment paper. Position a rack in the middle of the oven and preheat the oven to 400°F.

Toss the gooseberries, granulated sugar, arrowroot, lemon zest and juice, allspice, and salt together in a large bowl. To assemble the galette, place the pastry round on the prepared baking sheet. Pour the filling in the middle of the pastry round and spread out to about 3 inches from the edge. Fold in the edges, pinching together tightly in a circle, but leave an opening in the center. Chill in the freezer for at least 15 minutes before baking. (See page 67 for more tips on shaping a galette.)

Brush the exposed crust with egg wash if desired, and sprinkle all over with demerara sugar. Bake on the middle rack of the oven until the crust is golden brown and the filling is bubbling throughout, 35 to 40 minutes.

Allow to cool on a wire rack for at least 30 minutes. Serve warm or at room temperature.

The galette will keep refrigerated for 3 days or at room temperature for 2 days.

gooseberry

Sweet Corn Custard Pie

Makes one 9-inch pie
Serves 8 to 10

This one is for our dad, the corn farmer of our family. No one could argue that midwesterners don't know their corn. The sweet corn that our dad grows is, as far as we're concerned, the best on the planet. You don't know sweet corn until you've eaten it straight from the field, lightly boiled or grilled and buttered, with a sprinkling of salt and pepper. We're taking it up a notch here and putting it in a pie. Almost savory, but definitely sweet, this is unquestionably a unique dessert.

All-Butter Crust for a 9-inch single-crust pie, partially prebaked (see pages 207 and 68)

As with fruit, the fresher and more local the sweet corn used for this pie, the better the flavor will come through. Plan to make this pie when sweet corn is in season.

3 cups fresh corn kernels (from 4 to 5 ears of corn)
2 tablespoons neutral vegetable oil
1 cup heavy cream
1¼ cups whole milk
6 tablespoons unsalted butter, melted
½ cup granulated sugar
2 tablespoons stone-ground yellow cornmeal
½ teaspoon kosher salt
½ cup light corn syrup
3 large eggs
1 yolk
1 tablespoon fresh lime juice

Position a rack in the center of the oven and preheat the oven to 425°F. Line a rimmed baking sheet with foil.

Combine the corn with the vegetable oil on the prepared baking sheet and roast until the corn is caramelized, 12 to 15 minutes, stirring occasionally. Be careful not to burn. In a blender (or using an immersion blender), combine the hot roasted corn, heavy cream, and whole milk, and puree. Allow the mixture to steep for at least 15 minutes. Reduce the oven temperature to 350°F.

Meanwhile, combine the melted butter with the sugar, cornmeal, salt, and corn syrup, and stir to combine. Stir in the eggs and yolk one at a time, mixing well after each addition. Stir in the lime juice.

Position a fine-mesh sieve so it rests on the edges of a steady bowl. Pour the corn mixture into the sieve and press with a spatula to remove the liquid. Continue to stir and press the corn until all the liquid is removed; there should be about 1 cup of yellow liquid with some small bits of corn throughout. Combine the liquid with the rest of the filling. Discard the corn.

Place the prebaked pie shell on a rimmed baking sheet, pour in the filling, and bake on the middle rack of the oven for 40 to 45 minutes, rotating 180 degrees when the edges start to set, 30 to 35 minutes through baking. The pie is finished when the edges are set and puffed slightly and the center is no longer liquid but still quite wobbly. Be careful not to overbake or the custard can separate. The filling will continue to cook and set after the pie is removed from the oven. Allow to cool completely on a wire rack, 2 to 3 hours. Serve slightly warm, at room temperature, or cool.

The pie will keep refrigerated for 2 days or at room temperature for 1 day.

Fall

Fall

When the air turns cool and the days get shorter, the first and foremost thing on our mind is apples. The Northeast's fall apple season is like no other— the quantity and variety of apples available here can't help but impress anyone who loves to bake pies with this beautiful fruit. We are lucky enough to get our apples locally from Wilklow Orchards. We ask them to provide us with two types of apples that are in season that will complement each other in our pies: one sweet and one tart. Every week during the season, we are blessed with a delicious combination from their orchard.

Along with apples, the fall months bring a variety of unique produce that includes some of our favorites, such as figs, black walnuts, Concord grapes, sweet potatoes, pumpkins, and pears. We add maple, honey, and molasses to many of our recipes for their warm, sweet notes, which perfectly reflect autumnal flavors.

Unexpected though it may seem, figs grow really well in Brooklyn. Supposedly the heat of the concrete and bricks that surround most brownstone backyards keeps the roots of the hearty fig trees just warm enough to ward off winter frost. We have a friend named Gabriel in the neighborhood of Red Hook who provides us with plump white figs every year, and we also source from California for beautiful Black Mission and Brown Turkey figs.

Black walnuts are sort of the black sheep of the walnut family. In their raw form, they have a distinctly medicinal note that could be termed "an acquired taste." Our enduring love for unexpected ingredients makes them exactly the kind of food we love to work with.

We can't talk about fall without giving Thanksgiving its due praise. It is hands-down the most exciting and hectic holiday at the pie shop. It is a particularly special time to us because Thanksgiving is truly synonymous with pie. It is a marathon week of baking: the oven stays on for twenty-four hours straight, four days in a row, and we work to churn out as many pies as we possibly can. Every Thanksgiving we've been in business, we've had customers lining up outside our doors as early as five a.m. to get their pies, and we sell out almost immediately. It is a special time to be working in the pie shop, a time when we catch up with neighbors and friends and reflect on the year that is coming to a close.

Salted Caramel Apple Pie

Makes one 9-inch pie
Serves 8 to 10

We make this pie every day of the week. Every single day. It's popular and approachable because it's made with seasonal, local apples and salted caramel—which are both delicious in their own right. However, by design it is neither heavy on the caramel nor heavy on the sea salt; they are supporting actors to the tangy apples and the buttery, thick crust. This is simply a really good apple pie—the kind of apple pie you could eat every day. Use a blend of sweet apples and tart apples—an easy combination is Granny Smith with Golden Delicious; however, if you are sourcing from your local orchard, ask them to recommend a sweet softer apple and a tart firmer apple.

All-Butter Crust for a 9-inch double-crust pie (see page 207)

1 cup plus 2 tablespoons granulated sugar

¼ cup water

¼ pound (1 stick) unsalted butter

½ cup heavy cream

2 lemons

6 to 7 baking apples (about 2½ pounds)

2 to 3 dashes Angostura bitters

⅓ cup raw sugar

¼ teaspoon ground cinnamon

¼ teaspoon ground allspice

Pinch freshly grated nutmeg

One grind fresh black pepper

¼ teaspoon kosher salt

2 tablespoons unbleached all-purpose flour

¼ teaspoon flake sea salt, plus more for finishing

Egg wash (1 large egg whisked with 1 teaspoon water and a pinch of salt)

Demerara sugar, for finishing

Sweating the apples in sugar and lemon juice before assembling the pie is a necessary step; it releases some of the excess moisture in the fruit and creates a less watery apple pie.

This recipe makes more caramel sauce than you will need; the larger proportions make it easier to avoid burning. Keep the rest in the fridge for up to 3 weeks; rewarm it to make ice cream sundaes.

Have ready and refrigerated one pastry-lined 9-inch pie pan and lattice strips to top (see pages 56 and 58).

Whisk together 1 cup of the granulated sugar and the water in a medium saucepan, and cook over medium-low heat until the sugar is just dissolved. Add the butter and bring to a slow boil. Continue cooking over medium heat until the mixture turns a deep golden brown, almost copper. Remove from the heat and immediately but slowly add the heavy cream—be careful, the mixture will bubble rapidly and steam. Whisk the final mixture together well and set aside to cool while you prepare the apple filling.

(recipe continues)

Juice the lemons into a large mixing bowl, removing any seeds. Prepare the apples using an apple-peeling machine, or core, peel, and thinly slice them with a sharp knife or on a mandoline. Dredge the apple slices in the lemon juice. Sprinkle lightly with the remaining 2 tablespoons granulated sugar. Set aside to soften slightly and release some of the juices, 20 to 30 minutes.

In a small bowl, sprinkle the Angostura bitters over the raw sugar. Add the cinnamon, allspice, nutmeg, black pepper, kosher salt, and flour, and mix well. Add the prepared apples to the sugar-spice mixture, leaving behind any excess liquids. Gently turn the apples to evenly distribute the spice mix.

Tightly layer the apples in the prepared pie shell so that there are minimal gaps, mounding the apples slightly higher in the center. Pour a generous ½ cup to ¾ cup of the caramel sauce evenly over the apples (use the larger quantity of sauce if you'd like a sweeter pie). Sprinkle with ¼ teaspoon of the flake sea salt. Assemble the lattice on top of the pie and crimp the edges as desired (see pages 58 and 64).

Chill the pie in the refrigerator for 10 to 15 minutes to set the pastry. Meanwhile, position the oven racks in the bottom and center positions, place a rimmed baking sheet on the bottom rack, and preheat the oven to 400°F.

Brush the pastry with the egg wash to coat, being careful not to drag the caramel onto the pastry (it will burn), and sprinkle with the desired amount of demerara sugar and flake sea salt. Place the pie on the rimmed baking sheet on the lowest rack of the oven. Bake for 20 to 25 minutes, or until the pastry is set and beginning to brown. Lower the oven temperature to 375°F, move the pie to the center oven rack, and continue to bake until the pastry is a deep golden brown and the juices are bubbling, 30 to 35 minutes longer. Test the apples for doneness with a skewer or sharp knife; they should be tender and should offer just the slightest resistance.

Allow to cool completely on a wire rack, 2 to 3 hours. Serve slightly warm or at room temperature.

The pie will keep refrigerated for 3 days or at room temperature for 2 days.

Plum Fig Pie

There is a time in the fall when figs and plums overlap—seize the opportunity to combine these two earthy fruits to make a pie that is as rich in color as it is in taste.

Makes one 9-inch pie
Serves 8 to 10

All-Butter Crust for a 9-inch double-crust pie (see page 207)

This pie is also delicious when topped with our Oat Crumble topping (see page 216).

1½ pounds fresh plums, cut into ¼-inch slices (3 cups)
1 pound fresh figs, halved (2 to 3 cups)
Pinch finely grated lemon zest
2 tablespoons fresh lemon juice
½ teaspoon ground ginger
¼ teaspoon ground allspice
Pinch ground cloves
½ teaspoon kosher salt
Dash Angostura bitters
Egg wash (1 large egg whisked with 1 teaspoon water and a pinch of salt)
Demerara sugar, for finishing

Have ready and refrigerated one pastry-lined 9-inch pie pan and pastry round or lattice to top (see pages 56 and 58).

Combine the plums, figs, lemon zest and juice, ginger, allspice, cloves, salt, and bitters in a large bowl, and stir well. Pour the filling into the refrigerated pie shell, arrange the lattice or pastry round on top, and crimp as desired (see pages 58 and 64).

Chill the pie in the refrigerator for 10 to 15 minutes to set the pastry. Meanwhile, position the oven racks in the bottom and center positions, place a rimmed baking sheet on the bottom rack, and preheat the oven to 425°F.

Brush the pastry with the egg wash to coat; if your pie has a lattice top, be careful not to drag the filling onto the pastry (it will burn). Sprinkle with the desired amount of demerara sugar.

Place the pie on the rimmed baking sheet on the lowest rack of the oven. Bake for 20 to 25 minutes, or until the pastry is set and beginning to brown. Lower the oven temperature to 375°F, move the pie to the center oven rack, and continue to bake until the pastry is a deep golden brown and the juices are bubbling throughout, 30 to 35 minutes longer.

Allow to cool completely on a wire rack, 2 to 3 hours. Serve slightly warm or at room temperature.

The pie will keep refrigerated for 3 days or at room temperature for 2 days.

Bourbon Pear Crumble Pie

Pears, like apples, are a great vehicle for a variety of flavors, and bourbon goes ever so nicely with the sweet flesh of a just ripened pear. To make the perfect pear pie, use pears that are neither underripe nor overripe—they should be slightly firm to the touch but not rock hard.

All-Butter Crust for a 9-inch single-crust pie (see page 207)

2 cups Oat Crumble (see page 216), to top

You can use an apple-peeling machine or a peeler and mandoline to prep the pears if they are the correct ripeness; if they are too soft, these tools will not work (it will be obviously and painfully difficult).

1 lemon
6 to 7 medium pears (enough for about 5 cups sliced)
2 tablespoons granulated sugar
2/3 cup packed light brown sugar
2 tablespoons all-purpose flour
1/2 teaspoon ground ginger
1/4 teaspoon ground allspice
1/8 teaspoon ground white pepper
1/2 teaspoon kosher salt
3 tablespoons bourbon (we like Buffalo Trace brand)
2 dashes Old Fashion bitters
1/2 teaspoon vanilla extract

Have ready and refrigerated one crimped 9-inch pie shell (see page 56) and oat crumble to top.

Juice the lemon into a large bowl, removing any seeds. Prepare the pears using an apple-peeling machine, or core, peel, and thinly slice them with a sharp knife or on a mandoline. Dredge the pear slices in the lemon juice. Sprinkle with the granulated sugar. Set aside to soften slightly and release some of the juices, 20 to 30 minutes. Meanwhile, position the oven racks in the bottom and center positions, place a rimmed baking sheet on the bottom rack, and preheat the oven to 425°F.

In a small bowl, stir together the brown sugar, flour, ginger, allspice, white pepper, and salt. Drain any excess juices from the pears. Toss the pears with the sugar mixture. Sprinkle with the bourbon, bitters, and vanilla. Tightly layer the pears in the prepared pie shell so that there are minimal gaps, mounding them slightly higher in the center. Top with the oat crumble.

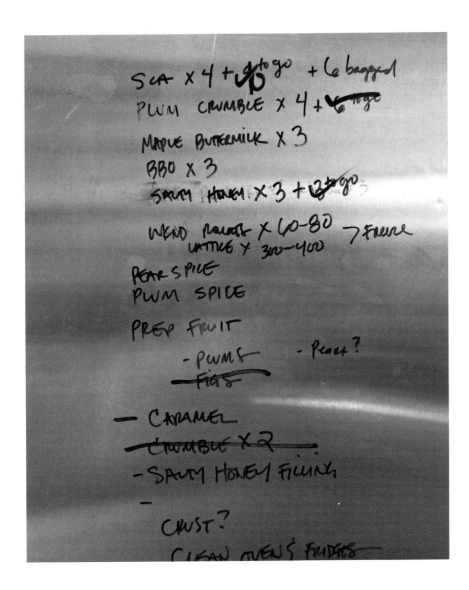

SEA x 4 + 15 to go + 6 bagged
PLUM CRUMBLE x 4 + 6 to go
MAPLE BUTTERMILK x 3
BBO x 3
SALTY HONEY x 3 + 13 to go

WKND PARROT x 60-80
LATTICE x 300-400   > FREEZE

PEAR SPICE
PLUM SPICE

PREP FRUIT
   - PLUMS   - PEARS?
   - FIGS

— CARAMEL
CRUMBLE x 2
- SALTY HONEY FILLING
   —
CRUST?
CLEAN OVENS FRIDGES

Place the pie on the rimmed baking sheet on the lowest rack of the oven. Bake for 20 to 25 minutes, or until the pastry is set and beginning to brown. Lower the oven temperature to 375°F, move the pie to the center oven rack, and continue to bake until the pastry is a deep golden brown and the juices are bubbling, 30 to 35 minutes longer. Test the pears with a skewer or sharp knife; they should be tender.

Allow to cool completely on a wire rack, 2 to 3 hours. Serve slightly warm or at room temperature.

The pie will keep refrigerated for 3 days or at room temperature for 2 days.

Concord Grape Pie

Makes one 10-inch tart
Serves 8 to 10

The intense grape flavor of Concords is like that of no other grape, and the appearance of their rich purple skin on the vine truly speaks to the beginning of fall.

All-Butter Crust for a 10-inch double-crust pie (see page 207)

This pie is baked in a tart pan to make room for the abstract triangle top crust. To achieve this shape, roll out your top crust in a large circle and cut free-form triangles and shapes. Arrange them on top of the filling so as to cover most of the pie. Brush on the egg wash and sprinkle with sugar as you like.

2 pounds Concord grapes, stemmed
Pinch finely grated lemon zest
1 tablespoon fresh lemon juice
½ cup granulated sugar
½ cup light brown sugar
3 tablespoons ground arrowroot
½ teaspoon allspice
½ teaspoon kosher salt
1 large egg
2 dashes Angostura bitters
Egg wash (1 large egg whisked with 1 teaspoon water and a pinch of salt)
Demerara sugar, for finishing

Have ready and refrigerated one pastry-lined 10-inch tart pan (see page 57) and pastry triangles or a 10-inch pastry round to top.

Squeeze the pulp out of each grape to separate the skin. Finely chop the skins, put them in a large bowl, and position a fine-mesh sieve on the rim. In a heavy-bottomed saucepan over medium-low heat, simmer the pulp until soft, stirring occasionally, about 10 minutes. Pour the pulp into the sieve and press through with a spatula to remove the seeds. Allow to cool slightly, about 10 minutes. Position the oven racks in the bottom and center positions, place a rimmed baking sheet on the bottom rack, and preheat the oven to 400°F.

Stir the lemon zest and juice, granulated and brown sugars, arrowroot, allspice, and salt into the grapes, followed by the egg and bitters. Pour the filling into the prepared tart shell and arrange the pastry triangles or round on top. Brush the pastry with the egg wash to coat, being careful not to drag the filling onto the pastry (it will burn). Sprinkle with the desired amount of demerara sugar.

Place the pie on the rimmed baking sheet on the lowest rack of the oven. Bake for 20 to 25 minutes, or until the pastry is set and beginning to brown. Lower the oven temperature to 350°F, move the pie to the center oven rack, and continue to bake until the pastry is a deep golden brown and the juices are bubbling throughout, 40 to 50 minutes longer.

Allow to cool completely on a wire rack, 2 to 3 hours. Serve slightly warm or at room temperature. The pie will keep refrigerated for 3 days or at room temperature for 2 days.

Salty Honey Pie

Salty Honey Pie is not for the faint of heart. It is a full-flavored, sweet, and yes, salty pie that for some of our customers has become an addiction. This pie actually resulted from a kitchen experiment. Emily was making a bourbon chess pie from an old recipe that she wanted to test, only to discover she was totally out of bourbon. So in place of the bourbon, she added some honey—well, a lot of honey. The pie puffed up like a marshmallow and seemed like it would never set, but she left it in long enough that the top became a toasty brown and the center was set into a golden rich custard. And boy, was it sweet! After a few tastes with the kitchen crew, Sophie Kamin, one of our pastry cooks at the time, reached for the flake sea salt and sprinkled a little on. It helped balance the sweetness perfectly. Salty Honey quickly became one of our most popular pies.

Makes one 9-inch pie
Serves 8 to 10

All-Butter Crust for a 9-inch single-crust pie (see page 207), crimped (see page 64) and frozen

¼ pound (1 stick) unsalted butter, melted

¾ cup granulated sugar

1 tablespoon white cornmeal

½ teaspoon kosher salt

1 teaspoon vanilla paste (Nielsen-Massey makes a readily available one)

¾ cup honey

3 large eggs

½ cup heavy cream

2 teaspoons white vinegar

1 to 2 teaspoons flake sea salt, for finishing

A variety of sea salts are increasingly available on the market, though we like flake Maldon; feel free to try different salts as the topping.

Have ready and frozen one pastry-lined 9-inch pie pan, crimped (see pages 56 and 64).

Position a rack in the center of the oven and preheat the oven to 375°F.

In a medium bowl, stir together the melted butter, sugar, cornmeal, salt, and vanilla paste. Stir in the honey and the eggs one at a time, followed by the heavy cream and vinegar.

Place the frozen pie shell on a rimmed baking sheet and strain the filling through a fine-mesh sieve directly into the pie shell, or strain it into a separate bowl and then pour it into the shell. Bake on the middle rack of the oven for 45 to 50 minutes, rotating 180 degrees when the edges start to set, 30 to 35 minutes through baking. The pie is finished when the edges are set and puffed up high and the center is no longer liquid but looks set like gelatin and is golden brown on top. Allow to cool completely on a wire rack, 2 to 3 hours. Sprinkle with flake sea salt. Serve slightly warm or at room temperature.

The pie will keep refrigerated for 4 days or at room temperature for 2 days.

Honeyed Fig Crumble Pie

Makes one 9-inch pie
Serves 8 to 10

Fresh figs make a delicious, rich pie filling. We use black, brown, or white figs, or a blend of all three. Adding honey and a crispy crumble topping takes this fig pie to a whole new dimension.

All-Butter Crust for a 9-inch single-crust pie (see page 207)

2 cups Oat Crumble (see page 216), to top

We specify a crumble topping here, but a lattice or full top works very nicely with this pie as well.

1½ to 2 pounds fresh figs, halved (5 cups)
2 tablespoons fresh lemon juice
1 tablespoon potato starch
½ teaspoon kosher salt
¾ cup honey
Dash Old Fashion bitters

Have ready and refrigerated one crimped 9-inch pie shell (see pages 56 and 64) and oat crumble to top. Position the oven racks in the bottom and center positions, place a rimmed baking sheet on the bottom rack, and preheat the oven to 425°F.

In a small bowl toss together the figs, lemon juice, potato starch, and salt. Drizzle with the honey and bitters and toss to coat. Pour the filling into the prepared shell and top with the oat crumble.

Place the pie on the rimmed baking sheet on the lowest rack of the oven. Bake for 20 to 25 minutes, or until the pastry is set and beginning to brown. Lower the oven temperature to 375°F, move the pie to the center oven rack, and continue to bake until the pastry is a deep golden brown and the juices are bubbling, 30 to 35 minutes longer.

Allow to cool completely on a wire rack, 2 to 3 hours. Serve slightly warm or at room temperature.

The pie will keep refrigerated for 3 days or at room temperature for 2 days.

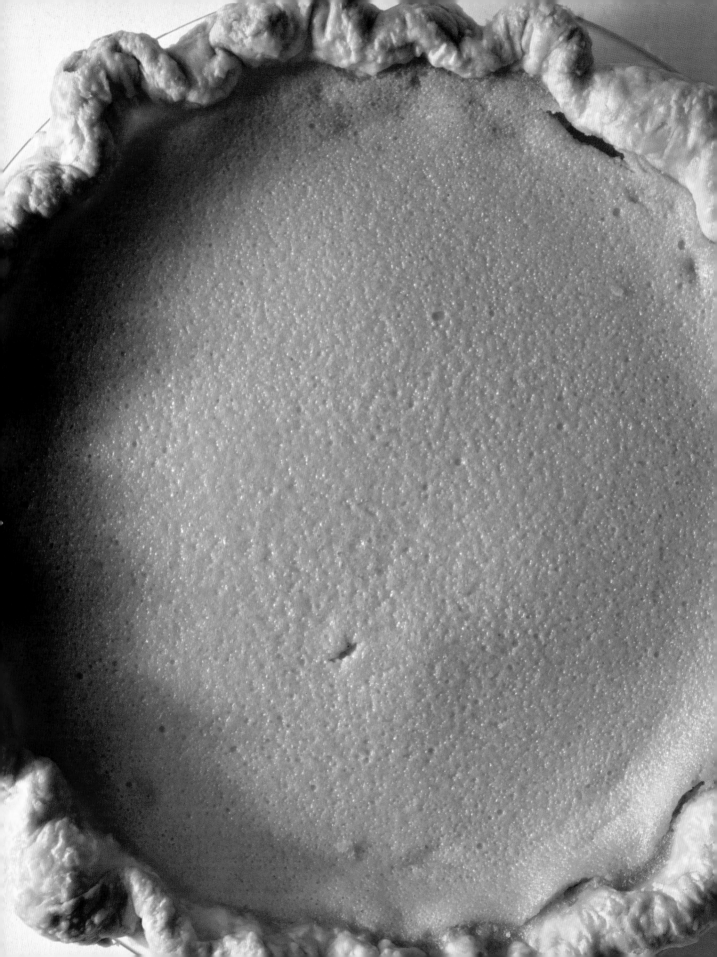

Maple Buttermilk Custard Pie

Maple collection happens in late winter, just as the ice begins to melt, so technically, maple syrup is an ingredient that comes about in early spring, but we love using this flavor in the fall. We like to use Grade B syrup for its more robust maple flavor. There are three A grades of maple syrup: light amber, medium amber, and dark amber. After dark amber comes Grade B. This very dark syrup has a stronger maple flavor than Grade A and is great for cooking. Regardless of grade, make sure you use pure fresh maple syrup—never imitation—for this recipe.

Makes one 9-inch pie
Serves 8 to 10

Cornmeal Crust for a 9-inch single-crust pie (see page 211), partially prebaked (see page 68)

1 tablespoon unbleached all-purpose flour

1 tablespoon stone-ground white cornmeal

¼ cup packed light brown sugar

½ teaspoon kosher salt

5 tablespoons unsalted butter, melted

1 teaspoon vanilla paste (or vanilla extract)

1 cup sour cream

3 large eggs

1 large egg yolk

¾ cup maple syrup (preferably Grade B)

1 cup buttermilk

We love Poorfarm Farm's small-batch, hand-harvested maple syrup from Vermont, and you, too, can order directly from them. See our "Sourcing" section for more information.

Position a rack in the center of the oven and preheat the oven to 325°F. Place the prebaked pie shell on a rimmed baking sheet.

In a large bowl, mix together the flour, cornmeal, brown sugar, salt, and melted butter. Add the vanilla paste (or vanilla extract) and the sour cream and stir until smooth. Add the eggs and egg yolk one at a time, blending well after each addition. Add the maple syrup and buttermilk and mix until smooth.

Strain the filling through a fine-mesh sieve directly into the pie shell, or strain it into a separate bowl and then pour it into the shell. Bake on the middle rack of the oven for 45 to 55 minutes, rotating 180 degrees when the edges start to set, 30 to 35 minutes through baking. The pie is finished when the edges are set and puffed slightly and the center is no longer liquid but still quite wobbly. Be careful not to overbake or the custard can separate; the filling will continue to cook and set after the pie is removed from the oven. Allow to cool completely on a wire rack, 2 to 3 hours. Serve slightly warm, at room temperature, or cool.

The pie will keep refrigerated for 2 days or at room temperature for 1 day.

Sour Cream Raisin Pie

Makes one 9-inch pie
Serves 8 to 10

Our grandmother regularly made this classic midwestern pie, and it was a favorite at our mother's restaurant in Hecla, South Dakota. We follow our grandmother's recipe here almost to the letter. Our only addition is to soak the raisins in a little allspice dram after plumping them with hot water; it adds a nice warmth and cuts the raisins' sweetness.

All-Butter Crust for a 9-inch single-crust pie (see page 207), fully prebaked (see page 69)

If you can't find allspice dram (we like St. Elizabeth brand), try spiced rum or any type of spiced liqueur you can find.

1 cup raisins, chopped
3 tablespoons allspice dram or other liqueur (optional)*
1½ cups sour cream
1 cup whole milk
½ cup packed light brown sugar
¼ cup granulated sugar
2 tablespoons plus 1 teaspoon cornstarch
½ teaspoon kosher salt
2 tablespoons fresh lemon juice
2 large egg yolks
1 large egg
4 tablespoons (½ stick) unsalted butter
1 cup heavy cream
2 tablespoons confectioners' sugar
½ teaspoon vanilla extract

In a large heatproof bowl, cover the chopped raisins with boiling water and allow to plump for 10 minutes. Drain well. Pour back into the bowl and sprinkle with allspice dram (if using). Position a fine-mesh sieve on the rim.

In a large heavy-bottomed saucepan, whisk together the sour cream, milk, brown and granulated sugars, cornstarch, salt, and lemon juice. Bring to a boil over medium heat, stirring occasionally. Reduce the heat to medium-low and continue to simmer for 2 minutes longer, stirring constantly.

Whisk the egg yolks and egg in a small bowl. Slowly whisk in about 1 cup of the hot sour cream mixture to temper the yolks. Add the yolk mixture back to the saucepan, return the mixture to a boil, and cook for 1 minute, stirring constantly. Remove from heat.

Immediately pour the filling into the sieve and use a spatula to press through and scrape any filling clinging to the bottom of the sieve. Stir together with the raisins and allow the filling to cool for about 10 minutes, stirring occasionally to prevent a skin from forming.

Stir in the butter 1 tablespoon at a time, fully incorporating each addition before adding the next. Pour into the prepared crust and press a piece of plastic wrap directly onto the surface of the filling. Refrigerate until firm, about 4 hours.

Just before serving, in the chilled bowl of an electric mixer beat the cream on medium speed until soft peaks form. Add the confectioners' sugar and vanilla and continue beating on medium-low speed just until the cream holds stiff peaks. Remove the plastic wrap from the surface of the filling and spread the cream over the pie. Slice and serve.

The pie will keep refrigerated for 2 days.

* If using a liqueur other than allspice dram (or none at all), add ¼ teaspoon ground allspice and ¼ teaspoon ground cinnamon when adding the salt.

Pear Anise Pie

Makes one 9-inch pie
Serves 8 to 10

Anise can be a controversial flavor note; it seems that people either love it or hate it. When paired with pears, however, the earthy sweet aroma of the anise elevates the delicate sweetness of the fruit in a perfect balance of flavors.

All-Butter Crust for a 9-inch double-crust pie (see page 207)

We use a little Peychaud's bitters in this pie for the aromatic anise flavor. Star anise can be used as a decorative element on the top as well.

1 lemon
6 to 7 medium pears (enough for about 5 cups sliced)
½ cup plus 2 tablespoons granulated sugar
1½ teaspoons anise seeds
¼ cup packed light brown sugar
2 tablespoons all-purpose flour
¼ teaspoon ground allspice
½ teaspoon kosher salt
2 dashes Peychaud's bitters
Egg wash (1 large egg whisked with 1 teaspoon water and a pinch of salt)
Demerara sugar, for finishing

Have ready and refrigerated one pastry-lined 9-inch pie pan and pastry round or lattice to top (see pages 56 and 58).

Juice the lemon into a large bowl, removing any seeds. Prepare the pears using an apple-peeling machine, or core, peel, and thinly slice them with a sharp knife or on a mandoline. Dredge the pear slices in the lemon juice. Sprinkle with 2 tablespoons of the granulated sugar. Set aside to soften slightly and release some of the juices, 20 to 30 minutes.

Toast the anise seeds in a skillet over medium heat until fragrant, about 5 minutes. In the bowl of a food processor fitted with the blade attachment, combine the remaining ½ cup granulated sugar, anise seeds, brown sugar, flour, allspice, salt, and bitters; process until the anise seeds are chopped. Shake the sugar mixture through a fine-mesh sieve to remove the anise seed hulls.

Drain any excess juices from the pears and toss the pears with the sugar mixture. Tightly layer the pears in the prepared pie shell so that there are minimal gaps, mounding them slightly higher in the center. Arrange the lattice or pastry round on top and crimp as desired (see pages 58 and 64).

Chill the pie in the refrigerator for 10 to 15 minutes to set the pastry. Meanwhile, position the oven racks in the bottom and center positions, place a rimmed baking sheet on the bottom rack, and preheat the oven to 425°F.

Brush the pastry with the egg wash to coat, and sprinkle with the desired amount of demerara sugar. Place the pie on the rimmed baking sheet on the lowest rack of the oven. Bake for 20 to 25 minutes, or until the pastry is set and beginning to brown. Lower the oven temperature to 375°F, move the pie to the center oven rack, and continue to bake until the pastry is a deep golden brown and the juices are bubbling, 30 to 35 minutes longer. Test the pears with a skewer or sharp knife; they should be tender.

Allow to cool completely on a wire rack, 2 to 3 hours. Serve slightly warm or at room temperature.

The pie will keep refrigerated for 3 days or at room temperature for 2 days.

Black Walnut Pie

The texture and appearance of this pie are similar to those of a traditional pecan pie, but instead it's made with an apple cider caramel. The floral fruitiness of the apple cider complements the robust flavor of the nuts.

Makes one 9-inch pie
Serves 8 to 10

Cornmeal Crust for a single-crust tart (see page 211), partially prebaked in a 9-inch springform pan (see pages 44 and 68)

1 cup black walnuts

1 cup granulated sugar

6 tablespoons unsalted butter

2 tablespoons water

¾ cup apple cider

2 teaspoons cider vinegar

½ teaspoon kosher salt

¼ teaspoon ground cinnamon

½ teaspoon ground ginger

2 teaspoons stone-ground cornmeal

3 large eggs

If you don't have a local source for black walnuts, see our "Sourcing" section (see page 41) for information about online ordering. This recipe also works well with traditional walnuts, or a mix of the two types.

Position a rack in the center of the oven and preheat the oven to 350°F. To toast the black walnuts, spread them in a single layer on a rimmed baking sheet and place in the oven for 5 to 7 minutes, or until fragrant, stirring occasionally. Pour into a shallow dish to cool.

Combine the sugar, butter, and water in a heavy-bottomed saucepan. Cook over medium-high heat until deep golden brown, 5 to 8 minutes, or until a candy thermometer reads 225°F. Turn off the heat and slowly pour in the apple cider; the caramel will bubble rapidly and steam. Add the cider vinegar and whisk until smooth.

Pour the caramel into a large bowl and allow to cool to the touch, at least 5 minutes. Whisk in the salt, cinnamon, ginger, and cornmeal. Whisk the eggs in a separate bowl. Slowly stream about ⅓ cup of the warm cider mixture into the eggs to temper. Add the cider-egg mixture back to the bowl. Stir in the toasted walnuts.

Place the prebaked tart shell on a rimmed baking sheet and pour in the filling. Bake on the middle rack of the oven for 25 to 30 minutes, rotating 180 degrees when the edges start to set, about 20 minutes through baking. The pie is finished when the edges are set and puffed slightly and the center is no longer liquid but still quite wobbly. Be careful not to overbake, or the custard can separate; the filling will continue to cook and set after the pie is removed from the oven. Allow to cool completely on a wire rack, 1 to 2 hours. Serve slightly warm, at room temperature, or cool. The pie will keep refrigerated for 3 days or at room temperature for 2 days.

Brown Butter Pumpkin Pie

Makes one 9-inch pie
Serves 8 to 10

In the pie shop we are often asked if we roast our own pumpkins for our pies. Some bakers do, but we've found that the consistency and texture of good canned pumpkin is far more reliable, not to mention the shortcut on labor. This is one instance where we will gladly open a can to make a pie filling. Since it's technically a custard, a smooth and creamy consistency is the goal, and processing the pumpkin helps break up any fibers for a smoother filling. The addition of browned butter gives the pumpkin a subtle butterscotch note that makes for the perfect autumnal pie.

All-Butter Crust for a 9-inch single-crust pie (see page 207), partially prebaked (see page 68)

If you want to use your own fresh pumpkin or squash, by all means give it a try. Ask at your farmers' market for a suggestion of which variety to use. Roast it in the oven until fork tender, scrape the flesh from the skin, and puree in food processor or blender. Use the same amount of fresh puree as the recipe calls for canned.

6 tablespoons unsalted butter

1 cup light brown sugar

2 tablespoons water

½ cup heavy cream

½ teaspoon vanilla extract

2 large eggs

2 large egg yolks

½ teaspoon kosher salt

1⅔ cups pumpkin puree

½ teaspoon ground allspice

½ teaspoon ground cinnamon

¼ teaspoon ground ginger

Pinch ground cloves

1 teaspoon molasses

2 teaspoons fresh lemon juice

⅔ cup whole milk

⅓ cup carrot juice

In a heavy-bottomed skillet, melt the butter over medium-low heat. Continue to cook; the butter will foam and then begin to turn golden, then nut brown; whisk occasionally. When the butter is nut brown, immediately add the brown sugar, whisk, and then carefully add the water to loosen. Bring the mixture to a boil and continue simmering until a candy thermometer reads 225°F. (If you don't have a candy thermometer, cook until the mixture smells caramelized and starts to darken.) Remove from the heat and slowly add the heavy cream (the mixture will bubble rapidly) and whisk until smooth. Allow to cool for at least 10 minutes. Stir in the vanilla extract.

Meanwhile, position a rack in the center of the oven and preheat the oven to 350°F. Place the prebaked pie shell on a rimmed baking sheet. In a separate bowl, lightly whisk the eggs and yolks together with the salt. Set aside.

In the bowl of a food processor fitted with the blade attachment or in a large bowl using an immersion blender, blend the pumpkin puree with the allspice, cinnamon, ginger, cloves, molasses, and lemon juice until smooth. With the machine running on low, stream the brown-butter butterscotch through the food processor's feed tube and process until combined. Stream in the egg mixture, followed by the milk and carrot juice; blend until smooth, stopping once or twice to scrape down the sides with a rubber scraper.

Strain the filling through a fine-mesh sieve into a separate bowl, pressing through with a rubber scraper. Pour into the prebaked shell. Bake on the middle rack of the oven for 45 to 55 minutes, rotating 180 degrees when the edges start to set, 30 to 35 minutes through baking. The pie is finished when the edges are set and puffed slightly and the center is no longer liquid but still quite wobbly. Be careful not to overbake or the custard can separate; the filling will continue to cook and set after the pie is removed from the oven. Allow to cool completely on a wire rack, 2 to 3 hours. Serve slightly warm, at room temperature, or cool.

The pie will keep refrigerated for 2 days or at room temperature for 1 day.

Sliced Sweet Potato & Apple Crumble Pie

Makes one 9-inch pie
Serves 8 to 10

While we know that sweet potatoes make a great custard pie, we wanted to create a pie where the potatoes are sliced, somewhat akin to candied sweet potatoes. Our first versions of this pie were a little too savory, so we added some sliced apple to lighten things up. Then we added a little fresh caramel, along with a hearty oat crumble top. This could easily be deemed the official afternoon snack pie.

All-Butter Crust for a 9-inch single-crust pie (see page 207), crimped and refrigerated

2 cups Oat Crumble (see page 216), to top, refrigerated

Use a juicy apple such as Cortland, Ida Red, or Golden Delicious, as it will provide extra moisture to the rather dry potatoes.

2 medium sweet potatoes (enough for about 2 cups sliced)
¾ cup granulated sugar
2 tablespoons water
6 tablespoons unsalted butter
¾ cup heavy cream
2 lemons
2 to 3 baking apples (enough for about 2 cups sliced)
¼ cup light brown sugar
¼ teaspoon ground allspice
¼ teaspoon ground ginger
½ teaspoon ground cinnamon
½ teaspoon kosher salt
1 teaspoon vanilla paste (Nielsen-Massey makes a readily available one)
Dash Angostura bitters

Have ready and refrigerated one pastry-lined 9-inch pie pan, crimped as desired (see pages 56 and 64) and crumble to top.

Peel the sweet potatoes, cover with cold water in a medium saucepan, and bring to a boil. Simmer until they are tender when tested with a sharp knife, but not fully cooked, about 20 minutes. Run under cold water to stop cooking. Set aside to soften slightly and release some of the juices, 20 to 30 minutes.

Whisk together the granulated sugar and water in a medium saucepan and cook over medium-low heat until the sugar is just dissolved. Add the butter and bring to a slow boil. Continue cooking over medium heat until the mixture turns a deep, golden brown, almost copper. Remove from the heat and immediately, but slowly, add the heavy cream—be careful, the mixture will bubble rapidly and steam. Whisk the final mixture together well and set aside to cool.

(recipe continues)

Position the oven racks in the bottom and center positions, place a rimmed baking sheet on the bottom rack, and preheat the oven to 425°F. Juice the lemons into a large bowl, removing any seeds. Prepare the apples using an apple-peeling machine, or core, peel, and thinly slice them with a sharp knife or on a mandoline until you have 2 cups of slices. Dredge the apple slices in the lemon juice.

Whisk together the brown sugar, allspice, ginger, cinnamon, and salt. Slice the cooled sweet potatoes into 1/8-inch slices using a mandoline or sharp knife, and measure out 2 cups slices. Combine the apple slices, brown sugar mixture, and the sweet potato slices and toss gently to incorporate.

Stir the vanilla paste and bitters into the cooled caramel. Pour the caramel over the apple mixture and stir gently to incorporate. Mound the filling into the refrigerated pie shell and evenly distribute the crumble on top.

Place the pie on the rimmed baking sheet on the lowest rack of the oven. Bake for 20 to 25 minutes, or until the pastry is set and beginning to brown. Lower the oven temperature to 375°F, move the pie to the center oven rack, and continue to bake until the pastry is a deep golden brown and the juices are bubbling throughout, 30 to 35 minutes longer.

Allow to cool completely on a wire rack, 2 to 3 hours. Serve slightly warm or at room temperature.

The pie will keep refrigerated for 3 days or at room temperature for 2 days.

Rosemary Honey Shoofly Pie

Shoofly pie is a traditional Pennsylvania Dutch recipe, traditionally made with molasses. We've swapped honey, and blended in fresh rosemary and a little brewed coffee, resulting in lighter, more aromatic flavor.

Makes one 9-inch pie
Serves 8 to 10

All-Butter Crust for a 9-inch single-crust pie (see page 207), partially prebaked (see page 68)

¾ cup granulated sugar

1 tablespoon rosemary leaves

1 cup all-purpose flour

¼ teaspoon kosher salt

½ teaspoon ground cinnamon

⅛ teaspoon ground cardamom

6 tablespoons unsalted butter, cut into ½-inch pieces

¾ cup honey

2 large eggs

½ cup whole milk

½ teaspoon kosher salt

2 teaspoons cider vinegar

½ teaspoon baking soda

½ cup strong brewed coffee, warm

The texture of this pie is almost like that of coffee cake, and that makes it a perfect treat for a weekend brunch or afternoon tea.

Position a rack in the center of the oven and preheat the oven to 350°F.

In the bowl of a food processor fitted with the blade attachment, combine the sugar and rosemary leaves and process until the rosemary is chopped into fine pieces. Add the flour, salt, cinnamon, cardamom, and butter and process to a coarse meal. Refrigerate until ready to use.

In a large bowl, beat together the honey and eggs. Mix in the milk, salt, and cider vinegar. Stir the baking soda into the warm coffee, and slowly stream into the honey mixture.

Place the prebaked pie shell on a rimmed baking sheet. Spread about one cup of the crumb mixture evenly in the bottom of the shell, gently pour the honey mixture over the top, and sprinkle on the remaining crumb mixture.

Bake on the middle rack of the oven for 45 to 55 minutes, rotating 180 degrees when the edges start to set, 30 to 35 minutes through baking. The pie is finished when the edges are set and puffed slightly and the center is slightly firm to the touch but still has some give. Be careful not to overbake or the custard can separate; the filling will continue to cook and set after the pie is removed from the oven. Allow to cool completely on a wire rack, 2 to 3 hours. Serve slightly warm or at room temperature. The pie will keep refrigerated for 2 days or at room temperature for 1 day.

Buttered Rum Cream Pie

Makes one 9-inch pie
Serves 8 to 10

In our quest to create a pie that highlights the perfect butterscotch flavor, we came upon a classic cocktail, hot buttered rum. Some recipes for this festive drink read practically like custard in a cup.

All-Butter Crust for a 9-inch single-crust pie (see page 207), fully prebaked (see page 69)

The trick to achieving a good butterscotch flavor is to not overcaramelize the brown sugar.

6 tablespoons unsalted butter

1 cup packed dark brown sugar

2 tablespoons water

1½ cups heavy cream

3 tablespoons cornstarch

½ teaspoon kosher salt

¼ teaspoon ground cinnamon

¼ teaspoon ground nutmeg

⅛ teaspoon ground cloves

2½ cups whole milk

4 large egg yolks

½ teaspoon vanilla paste (Nielsen-Massey makes a readily available one)

About 3 tablespoons dark rum (we like Gosling's brand)

2 tablespoons confectioners' sugar

½ teaspoon vanilla extract

In a heavy-bottomed saucepan, melt the butter over medium-low heat; have ready a small heatproof bowl. Continue to cook; the butter will foam and then begin to turn golden, then nut brown; whisk occasionally. When the butter is nut brown, remove from the heat and immediately pour it into the bowl. Add the brown sugar to the saucepan, whisk in the water to loosen the sugar, and add half the browned butter. Place the remaining brown butter in the freezer to solidify, 5 to 10 minutes.

Bring the brown sugar mixture to a boil over medium heat and continue to cook until the sugar just starts to smell caramelized, 4 to 5 minutes. Remove from heat and slowly add ½ cup of the heavy cream (the mixture will bubble rapidly) and whisk until smooth. Set aside.

In a small bowl, whisk together the cornstarch, salt, cinnamon, nutmeg, and cloves. Pour in about ¼ cup of the caramel and whisk to make a slurry. Add the slurry back to the caramel in the saucepan, and slowly whisk in the milk. Whisk the egg yolks together in a separate small bowl; set aside. Bring the mixture back to a boil over medium heat, stirring frequently. Once it's boiling, stir constantly and continue to cook for 2 minutes. Remove from the heat.

Slowly whisk about a cup of the hot filling into the yolks to temper them. Have a large bowl ready for cooling and a fine-mesh sieve to strain the mixture through. Add the yolk mixture back to the saucepan and cook over medium heat, stirring constantly, until the mixture just returns to a boil, 1 to 2 minutes. Strain through the sieve, using a spatula to push the mixture through and to scrape the filling clinging to the bottom of the sieve. Allow to cool for 10 minutes, stirring occasionally to prevent a skin from forming.

Meanwhile, remove the solidified butter from the freezer and whip with a fork.

Whisk the vanilla paste and rum to taste into the cooled filling, followed, in three additions, by the remaining butter, whisking until each one is incorporated before adding the next. Pour into the prebaked pie shell and press a piece of plastic wrap directly on top of the filling. Refrigerate until firm, at least 3 hours.

Before serving, whip the remaining 1 cup cream to soft peaks, add the confectioners' sugar and vanilla extract, and continue whipping just until the cream holds stiff peaks. Remove the plastic wrap from the filling, spread the cream over the filling, and refrigerate until serving.

The pie will keep refrigerated for up to 2 days.

Black Bottom Oatmeal Pie

Makes one 9-inch pie
Serves 8 to 10

This pie has slowly but surely become a sort of cult favorite in the pie shop. We loved it from the start for its oatmeal–chocolate chip cookie quality; it's like a pie version of that classic recipe. In olden days, this pie (minus the chocolate) was dubbed "poor man's pecan pie" because oats are far less expensive than pecans. We up the ante by adding a decadent layer of dark chocolate ganache on the bottom.

All-Butter Crust for a 9-inch single-crust pie (see page 207), partially prebaked (see page 68) and cooled

If you want to make this recipe without the chocolate on the bottom, by all means do; it will be delicious.

1½ cups rolled oats

¼ cup heavy cream

4 ounces bittersweet chocolate (we use 70%), chopped into ¼-inch pieces

¾ cup packed light brown sugar

¼ teaspoon ground ginger

½ teaspoon kosher salt

5 tablespoons unsalted butter, melted

1 cup dark corn syrup

1 teaspoon vanilla extract

2 teaspoons cider vinegar

4 large eggs

Position a rack in the center of the oven and preheat the oven to 350°F. Spread the oats on a rimmed baking sheet and toast in the oven for 10 to 12 minutes, stirring occasionally. Set aside to cool. Reduce the oven temperature to 325°F.

To make the ganache layer, bring the heavy cream just to a boil over medium heat in a heavy-bottomed saucepan. Remove from the heat and pour in the chocolate pieces. Swirl the cream around to distribute and cover the chocolate; let sit for 5 minutes. Whisk gently until smooth. Scrape the ganache into the cooled pie shell and spread evenly over the bottom. Place the shell in the freezer to set the ganache while making the filling.

In a large bowl, whisk together the brown sugar, ginger, salt, and melted butter. Add the corn syrup, vanilla, and cider vinegar and whisk to combine. Add the eggs one at a time, blending well after each addition. Stir in the cooled oats.

Place the ganache-coated pie shell on a rimmed baking sheet and pour in the filling. Bake on the middle rack of the oven for about 55 minutes, rotating 180 degrees when the edges start to set, 30 to 35 minutes through baking. The pie is finished when the edges are set and puffed slightly and the center is slightly firm to the touch but still has some give (like gelatin). Allow to cool completely on a wire rack, 2 to 3 hours. Serve slightly warm or at room temperature.

The pie will keep refrigerated for 3 days or at room temperature for 2 days.

Winter

Winter

Fresh ingredients are scarce during the winter, so one must get creative with what's on hand, whether baking dessert or feeding dinner to a crowd. For pie, we look with eager hearts to the West Coast for its abundance of citrus—some sweetness and color to work with in a world of cellared root vegetables (as much as we love them). We continue working with apples because we have access to them locally, and our creative custard quotient goes way up. Cranberries are a welcome burst of color, and our Cranberry Sage Pie is definitely one of our most popular during the winter months. Oftentimes this is when we test recipes, in the kitchen and on customers alike—chess pies being the foundation of many of our experiments.

We love chess pie so much for its creative possibilities that the name merits some description right here and now. It is said that chess pie had its humble beginnings on American soil in the plantation homes of the South, where butter and eggs were pantry staples. The third ingredient of choice in this most basic pie recipe is sugar—back in the day, molasses was often used (before refined sugars were on the market). The name "chess" is often credited to two things: the pie chest and, well, southern accents. Chess pie is composed largely of sugar, a natural preservative; thus, it holds up well without refrigeration (in a pie chest, for example), should you find yourself without a cooling source. And with its easy-to-find ingredients, it's "jes' pie"—simple as that. Sounds about right; during cold winter months, all we really want is just pie.

Cranberry Sage Pie

Makes one 9-inch pie
Serves 8 to 10

In the wintertime, colorful fruits, aside from citrus, are few and far between. Cranberries appear in early fall and are the perfect berry to pair with apples and pears, but we wanted to feature them in their own right. Sage often appears on a holiday table in roasted stuffing, but why not give it some attention in the dessert course?

All-Butter Crust for a 9-inch double-crust pie (see page 207)

This pie also works well with streusel topping in place of the lattice.

¾ cup dried cranberries
1 tablespoon coarsely chopped fresh sage
½ cup granulated sugar
½ cup packed light brown sugar
½ teaspoon kosher salt
4 tablespoons ground arrowroot
¼ teaspoon ground cinnamon
¼ teaspoon ground allspice
4 cups whole cranberries, fresh or frozen (two 10-ounce bags)
1 small baking apple, such as Northern Spy or Golden Delicious
1 tablespoon vanilla extract
1 large egg, lightly beaten
Egg wash (1 large egg whisked with 1 teaspoon water and a pinch of salt)
Demerara sugar, for finishing

Have ready and refrigerated one pastry-lined 9-inch pie pan and pastry round or lattice to top (see pages 56 and 58).

In a heatproof bowl, pour boiling water over the dried cranberries to cover by about an inch. Allow them to plump while making the remaining filling.

In a food processor fitted with the blade attachment, combine the chopped sage, granulated and brown sugars, salt, arrowroot, cinnamon, and allspice. Process until the sage is fully blended. Pour the sugar mixture into a large bowl.

Use the same food processor bowl to briefly process 2 cups of the whole cranberries to a rough chop; add them, along with the remaining 2 cups whole cranberries, to the sugar mixture.

Peel the apple and shred on the large holes of a box grater. In a colander, drain the plumped dried cranberries of excess water, but do not press or squeeze them out. Add the shredded apple and the drained dried cranberries to the bowl with the rest of the filling and mix well. Stir in the vanilla extract and egg, and mix well. Pour the filling into the refrigerated pie shell, arrange the lattice or pastry round on top, and crimp as desired (see pages 58 and 64).

Chill the pie in the refrigerator for 10 to 15 minutes to set the pastry. Meanwhile, position the oven racks in the bottom and center positions, place a rimmed baking sheet on the bottom rack, and preheat the oven to 425°F.

Brush the pastry with the egg wash to coat; if your pie has a lattice top, be careful not to drag the filling onto the pastry (it will burn). Sprinkle with the desired amount of demerara sugar.

Place the pie on the rimmed baking sheet on the lowest rack of the oven. Bake for 20 to 25 minutes, or until the pastry is set and beginning to brown. Lower the oven temperature to 375°F, move the pie to the center oven rack, and continue to bake until the pastry is a deep golden brown and the juices are bubbling throughout, 35 to 45 minutes longer.

Allow to cool completely on a wire rack, 2 to 3 hours. Serve slightly warm or at room temperature.

The pie will keep for 3 days refrigerated or for up to 2 days at room temperature.

Egg 'n' Grogg Pie

We created this pie for the holiday season—it's a little boozy, like egg nog, and has a classic holiday spice profile. It is officially the first pie with a crumb crust that we served in the pie shop, so it's got some claim to fame. In case you're curious, Egg 'n' Grogg is taken from the origins of the name "eggnog"—egg being the custardy cream, and nog (or grogg) the spirit pairing.

Makes one 9-inch pie
Serves 8 to 10

Gingersnap Crumb Crust for a 9-inch pie (see page 212)

¾ cup cream cheese, softened

¾ cup granulated sugar

¼ teaspoon kosher salt

½ teaspoon vanilla paste (Nielsen-Massey makes a readily available one)

½ teaspoon freshly grated nutmeg

¼ teaspoon ground allspice

¼ teaspoon ground cinnamon

Pinch ground cloves

3 large eggs

1 cup heavy cream

3 tablespoons dark rum

½ teaspoon fresh lemon juice

We use dark rum, but you can also use brandy or white or gold rum. Grate a little fresh nutmeg on top when the pie is cooled for an especially fragrant dessert.

Position a rack in the center of the oven and preheat the oven to 325°F. Place the prepared crumb shell on a rimmed baking sheet.

In the bowl of an electric mixer fitted with the paddle attachment, blend the softened cream cheese with the sugar, salt, vanilla paste, nutmeg, allspice, cinnamon, and cloves until well mixed. Beat in the eggs one at a time, followed by the heavy cream, rum, and lemon juice. Stir until well combined.

Carefully pour the filling into the pie shell; to avoid disturbing the crumb crust, slow the stream by pouring it over a rubber scraper and letting the filling dribble into the pan. Bake on the middle rack of the oven for 40 to 45 minutes, rotating 180 degrees when the edges start to set, about 25 minutes through baking. The pie is finished when the edges are set and the center is no longer liquid but still quite wobbly. Be careful not to overbake or the custard can separate; the filling will continue to cook and set after the pie is removed from the oven. Allow to cool completely on a wire rack, 2 to 3 hours. Serve slightly warm, at room temperature, or cool.

The pie will keep refrigerated for 2 days or at room temperature for 1 day.

Junipear Pie

Makes one 9-inch pie
Serves 8 to 10

Juniper trees are relatively common in North America; the berries that grow on their branches are wonderfully aromatic and most commonly used to flavor gin. This recipe is inspired by the gin-based cocktail named "the Bee's Knees" (thanks to our former pie baker Rick Visser for encouraging that idea). We get our juniper from our forager, but you can also source it from spice merchants or, if you are lucky, your own backyard—if you have access to a juniper tree, pick and dry some for yourself.

All-Butter Crust for a 9-inch double-crust pie (see page 207)

Use slightly firm but not hard (and definitely not overripe) pears to achieve the best texture when baked.

1 lemon
½ orange
6 to 7 medium pears (2½ to 3 pounds fresh)
½ cup plus 2 tablespoons granulated sugar
3 tablespoons all-purpose flour
1½ teaspoons dried juniper berries
½ teaspoon ground cinnamon
½ teaspoon kosher salt
Pinch finely grated lemon zest
¼ cup honey
Egg wash (1 large egg whisked with 1 teaspoon water and a pinch of salt)
Demerara sugar, for finishing

Have ready and refrigerated one pastry-lined 9-inch pie pan and pastry round or lattice to top (see pages 56 and 58).

Juice the lemon and orange into a large bowl, removing any seeds. Prepare the pears using an apple-peeling machine, or core, peel, and thinly slice them with a sharp knife or on a mandoline until you have about 5 cups sliced. Dredge the slices in the lemon and orange juice. Sprinkle lightly with 2 tablespoons of the granulated sugar. Set aside to soften slightly and release some of the juices, 20 to 30 minutes.

In the bowl of a food processor fitted with the blade attachment, combine the remaining ½ cup granulated sugar, flour, juniper berries, cinnamon, salt, and lemon zest; process until the juniper berries are chopped and fragrant. To remove any remaining large pieces of juniper berry, shake the sugar mixture through a fine-mesh sieve into a large bowl.

Leaving behind any excess juice, transfer the pears to the bowl together with the sugar mixture, add the honey, and toss to combine. Tightly layer the pears in the prepared pie shell so that there are minimal gaps, mounding them slightly higher in the center. Arrange the lattice or pastry round on top and crimp as desired (see pages 58 and 64).

Chill the pie in the refrigerator for 10 to 15 minutes to set the pastry. Meanwhile, position the oven racks in the bottom and center positions, place a rimmed baking sheet on the bottom rack, and preheat the oven to 425°F.

Brush the pastry with the egg wash to coat, and sprinkle with the desired amount of demerara sugar. Place the pie on the rimmed baking sheet on the lowest rack of the oven. Bake for 20 to 25 minutes, or until the pastry is set and beginning to brown. Lower the oven temperature to 375°F, move the pie to the center oven rack, and continue to bake until the pastry is a deep golden brown and the juices are bubbling, 30 to 35 minutes longer. Test the pears with a skewer or sharp knife; they should be tender.

Allow to cool completely on a wire rack, 2 to 3 hours. Serve slightly warm or at room temperature.

The pie will keep refrigerated for 3 days or at room temperature for 2 days.

Malted Chocolate Pecan Pie

Makes one 9-inch pie
Serves 8 to 10

We are lucky to have Brooklyn Homebrew as neighbors to the pie shop, not only because they provide us with our barley malt syrup (primarily used in beer brewing) for this pie, but they also share samples of their delicious brews with us! We suggest pairing this pie with a coffee stout for dessert.

All-Butter Crust for a 9-inch single-crust pie (see page 207), partially prebaked (see page 68)

1½ cups pecan pieces
4 tablespoons (½ stick) unsalted butter, melted
2 ounces bittersweet chocolate (55% cocoa)
1 cup packed light brown sugar
¼ cup barley malt syrup (see "Ingredients" section for sources)
¾ teaspoon kosher salt
½ teaspoon ground cinnamon
½ teaspoon ground ginger
½ cup sour cream
3 large eggs
1 large egg yolk

We like to use chopped pecans rather than whole; it creates a better balance of nuts to crust and filling. It's also easier to cut and easier to eat.

Position a rack in the center of the oven and preheat the oven to 350°F. To toast the pecans, spread them in a single layer on a rimmed baking sheet and place in the oven for 6 to 8 minutes, or until the nuts are fragrant, stirring occasionally. Set aside to cool.

Bring an inch of water to a simmer in a medium saucepan. Combine the butter and chocolate in a heatproof bowl large enough to rest on the rim of the saucepan, above the water. Melt the butter and chocolate over this double boiler, whisking occasionally until smooth. Remove from the heat. Add the brown sugar, barley malt syrup, salt, cinnamon, and ginger, and stir well. Mix in the sour cream, then the eggs and egg yolk one at a time, stirring briskly after each addition. Stir in the cooled toasted pecan pieces.

Place the prebaked pie shell on a rimmed baking sheet and pour in the filling. Bake on the middle rack of the oven for 52 to 57 minutes, rotating 180 degrees when the edges start to set, about 35 minutes through baking. The pie is finished when the edges are set and puffed slightly and the center is slightly firm to the touch but still has some wobble (like gelatin). Be careful not to overbake or the custard can separate; the filling will continue to cook and set after the pie is removed from the oven.

Allow to cool completely on a wire rack, 2 to 3 hours. Serve slightly warm or at room temperature. The pie will keep refrigerated for 3 days or at room temperature for 2 days.

Blushing Apple Pie

Makes one 9-inch pie
Serves 8 to 10

Beets are naturally rich in color and have an earthy, sweet flavor when roasted that pairs nicely with apples and lends the perfect blushing color to the fruit.

All-Butter Crust for a 9-inch double-crust pie (see page 207)

For a cheat on the beets, you can purchase a pack of precooked vacuum-sealed beets; use some for your pie, and save the rest for salad.

½ orange
6 to 7 baking apples (about 2½ pounds fresh)
¼ cup plus 2 tablespoons granulated sugar
½ cup packed light brown sugar
½ medium beet, oven roasted until tender and chopped into ½-inch dice
¼ teaspoon ground ginger
¼ teaspoon ground cardamom
½ teaspoon kosher salt
3 tablespoons all-purpose flour
1½ teaspoons vanilla paste (Nielsen-Massey makes a readily available one)
¼ teaspoon orange zest
1 tablespoon cider vinegar
1 to 2 dashes Angostura bitters
Egg wash (1 large egg whisked with 1 teaspoon water and a pinch of salt)
Demerara sugar, for finishing

Have ready and refrigerated one pastry-lined 9-inch pie pan and pastry round or lattice to top (see pages 56 and 58).

Juice the orange into a large bowl. Prepare the apples using an apple-peeling machine, or core, peel, and thinly slice them with a sharp knife or on a mandoline. Dredge the apple slices in the orange juice. Sprinkle lightly with 2 tablespoons of the granulated sugar. Set aside to soften slightly and release some of the juices, 20 to 30 minutes.

In the bowl of a food processor fitted with the blade attachment, combine the remaining ¼ cup granulated sugar, brown sugar, chopped beet, ginger, cardamom, salt, flour, vanilla paste, zest, vinegar, and bitters, and process until the beet is fully incorporated into the sugar.

Drain any excess liquid from the sliced apples, add the beet-sugar mixture, and toss the apples to coat them thoroughly. Tightly layer the apples in the prepared pie shell so that there are minimal gaps, mounding the apples slightly higher in the center. Arrange the lattice or pastry round on top and crimp as desired (see pages 58 and 64).

Chill the pie in the refrigerator for 10 to 15 minutes to set the pastry. Meanwhile, position the oven racks in the bottom and center positions, place a rimmed baking sheet on the bottom rack, and preheat the oven to 400°F.

Brush the pastry with the egg wash to coat; if your pie has a lattice top, be careful not to drag the filling onto the pastry (it will burn). Sprinkle with the desired amount of demerara sugar. Place the pie on a rimmed baking sheet on the lowest rack of the oven. Bake for 20 to 25 minutes, or until the pastry is set and beginning to brown. Lower the oven temperature to 375°F, move the pie to the center oven rack, and continue to bake until the pastry is a deep golden brown and the juices are bubbling throughout, 40 to 50 minutes longer.

Allow to cool completely on a wire rack, 2 to 3 hours. Serve slightly warm or at room temperature.

The pie will keep refrigerated for 3 days or at room temperature for 2 days.

Salt Pork Apple Pie

Makes one 9-inch pie
Serves 8 to 10

One of our first employees at the pie shop was a young woman named Ali Rudel. When she entered a pie competition where she knew we'd be the judges, she unearthed a recipe for Salt Pork Apple Pie from an old New England cookbook and tested and tweaked until it was a tasty pie she knew we would like. Though she got our vote, she didn't win the competition, but this pie is definitely a winner in our hearts.

All-Butter Crust for a 9-inch double-crust pie (see page 207)

Ali added maple sugar for a special sweetness. If you can't find maple sugar easily, just add a few tablespoons of maple syrup to granulated sugar. Ask your local butcher to provide you with salt pork or look for Niman Ranch brand.

6 to 7 baking apples (about 2½ pounds fresh)
3 tablespoons apple cider vinegar
2 tablespoons granulated sugar
1 cup maple sugar (or ¾ cup granulated sugar plus 3 tablespoons maple syrup)
½ teaspoon cinnamon
¼ teaspoon allspice
¼ teaspoon kosher salt
Dash Angostura bitters
3 tablespoons all-purpose flour
¼ to ½ pound salt pork (depending on fat content)
Egg wash (1 large egg whisked with 1 teaspoon water and a pinch of salt)
Demerara sugar, to finish

Have ready and refrigerated one pastry-lined 9-inch pie pan and pastry round or lattice to top (see pages 56 and 58).

Prepare the apples using an apple-peeling machine, or core, peel, and thinly slice them with a sharp knife or on a mandoline. Sprinkle the apple slices with the apple cider vinegar and the granulated sugar. Set aside to soften slightly and release some of the juices, 20 to 30 minutes.

In a medium bowl, combine the maple sugar, cinnamon, allspice, kosher salt, and bitters, and mix well; stir in the flour.

Slice the salt pork into ¼-inch pieces and cook in a skillet over medium heat to render the fat, 5 to 8 minutes. Strain through a fine-mesh sieve and allow to cool slightly.

Drain any excess liquid from the sliced apples and discard; add the spice mixture and toss the apples to coat them thoroughly. Add about 4 tablespoons of the rendered fat to the apple mixture.

Arrange half the apples in the pie shell and top with half the fresh salt pork slices. Repeat for a second layer of apples and salt pork. Arrange the lattice or pastry round on top and crimp as desired (see pages 58 and 64).

Chill the pie in the refrigerator for 10 to 15 minutes to set the pastry. Meanwhile, position the oven racks in the bottom and center positions, place a rimmed baking sheet on the bottom rack, and preheat the oven to 425°F.

Brush the pastry with the egg wash to coat, and sprinkle with the desired amount of demerara sugar. Place the pie on the rimmed baking sheet on the lowest rack of the oven. Bake for 20 to 25 minutes, or until the pastry is set and beginning to brown. Lower the oven temperature to 375°F, move the pie to the center oven rack, and continue to bake until the pastry is a deep golden brown and the juices are bubbling, 35 to 40 minutes longer. Test the apples for doneness with a skewer or sharp knife; they should be tender and offer just the slightest resistance.

Allow to cool completely on a wire rack, 2 to 3 hours. Serve slightly warm or at room temperature.

The pie will keep refrigerated for 3 days or at room temperature for 2 days.

Grapefruit Custard Pie

Admittedly, we like to cook with booze. We use our fair share of bourbon, maybe because Brooklyn folks like it so much, but we also love bitters—a main component of many good cocktails. Campari is a bitter aperitif, invented by an Italian well over one hundred years ago. Originally it was colored with dye that was derived from crushed bugs. Nowadays it has plain old food coloring in it, but it sure is perfect for adding a bitter note and a little color to our grapefruit custard pie.

Makes one 9-inch pie
Serves 8 to 10

All-Butter Crust for a 9-inch single-crust pie (see page 207), partially prebaked (see page 68)

1¼ cups granulated sugar

2 tablespoons all-purpose flour

½ teaspoon kosher salt

2 tablespoons unsalted butter, melted

3 large eggs

1 large egg yolk

1 cup freshly squeezed grapefruit juice (from about 2 grapefruits)

3 tablespoons Campari liqueur

1 cup heavy cream

Dash orange-flavor cocktail bitters (optional)

Don't hesitate to buy an entire bottle of Campari for this one recipe. If you like to imbibe, it's a delicious mixer for a variety of cocktails; our favorite is the Negroni.

Position a rack in the center of the oven and preheat the oven to 325°F. Place the prebaked pie shell on a rimmed baking sheet.

In a large bowl, whisk together the sugar, flour, salt, and melted butter. Whisk in the eggs and egg yolk one at a time, blending well after each addition. Whisk in the grapefruit juice, Campari, heavy cream, and bitters, if using.

Strain the filling through a fine-mesh sieve directly into the pie shell, or strain it into a separate bowl and then pour it into the shell. Bake on the middle rack of the oven for 50 to 55 minutes, rotating 180 degrees when the edges start to set, 30 to 35 minutes through baking. The pie is finished when the edges are set and puffed slightly and the center is no longer liquid but still quite wobbly. Be careful not to overbake or the custard can separate; the filling will continue to cook and set after the pie is removed from the oven. Allow to cool completely on a wire rack, 2 to 3 hours. Serve at room temperature or cool.

The pie will keep refrigerated for 2 days or at room temperature for 1 day.

Lemon Chess Pie

Makes one 9-inch pie
Serves 8 to 10

Lemon Chess has garnered a close following in the pie shop, appearing most often on the menu during the winter months, when fresh fruits are scarce on the East Coast and we source from the West Coast for its bounty of citrus. This tangy but rich custard is a longtime favorite of our pie shop customers.

All-Butter Crust for a 9-inch single-crust pie (see page 207), partially prebaked (see page 68)

This may seem obvious, but please use only freshly squeezed citrus juice for this pie. It's the main ingredient, after all.

Zest of 1 lemon
1⅔ cups granulated sugar
1 tablespoon stone-ground yellow cornmeal
1 tablespoon flour
½ teaspoon kosher salt
5 tablespoons unsalted butter, melted
5 large eggs
⅔ cup heavy cream
7 tablespoons fresh lemon juice (from about 3 lemons)
3 tablespoons fresh orange juice
½ teaspoon vanilla extract

Position a rack in the center of the oven and preheat the oven to 325°F. Place the prebaked pie shell on a rimmed baking sheet.

In large bowl, stir together the lemon zest, sugar, cornmeal, flour, and salt. Use a wooden spoon or spatula to stir in the melted butter, then the eggs one at a time, stirring well after each addition. Mix briskly until the filling is thick and light colored. Stir in the heavy cream, followed by the lemon juice, orange juice, and vanilla extract.

Strain the filling through a fine-mesh sieve directly into the pie shell, or strain it into a separate bowl and then pour it into the shell. Bake on the middle rack of the oven for 40 to 50 minutes, rotating 180 degrees when the edges start to set, 30 to 35 minutes through baking. The pie is finished when the edges are set and puffed slightly and the center is no longer liquid but still wobbles slightly; it should be lightly golden on top. Be careful not to overbake or the custard can separate; the filling will continue to cook and set as it cools. Allow to cool completely on a wire rack, 3 to 4 hours. Slice and serve.

The pie will keep refrigerated for 2 days or at room temperature for 1 day.

Black Bottom Lemon Pie

Meyer lemons are a particularly delicious and easy to find variety of lemon available during the dead of winter, when you really need to eat something life affirming. The richness of the dark chocolate layer on the bottom goes particularly well with the peppery, warm citrus flavor Meyer lemons offer. If you don't have Meyer lemons, you can use regular lemons, but the flavor won't be exactly the same.

Makes one 9-inch pie
Serves 8 to 10

All-Butter Crust for a 9-inch single-crust pie (see page 207), partially prebaked (see page 68) and cooled

¾ cup heavy cream

4 ounces bittersweet chocolate (we use 70% cocoa), chopped into ¼-inch pieces

4 large eggs

1 large egg yolk

1⅓ cups granulated sugar

½ teaspoon kosher salt

½ cup fresh Meyer lemon juice (from 3 to 4 lemons)

¼ cup fresh orange juice

Finely grated zest of 1 Meyer lemon

Finely grated zest of ¼ orange

If you have access to fresh mandarin oranges, this recipe is also excellent made with their juice. Reverse the lemon and orange quantities and reduce the sugar to taste, or by about ⅓ cup.

To make the ganache layer, bring ¼ cup of the heavy cream just to a boil over medium heat in a heavy-bottomed saucepan. Remove from the heat and pour in the chocolate pieces. Swirl the cream around to distribute and cover the chocolate. Let sit for 5 minutes, and then whisk gently to combine. Scrape the ganache into the cooled pie shell and spread evenly over the bottom and halfway up the sides. Refrigerate the shell to set the ganache while making the filling. Position a rack in the center of the oven and preheat the oven to 325°F.

In the bowl of an electric mixer fitted with the paddle attachment, combine the eggs, egg yolk, sugar, and salt, and mix on medium speed until thick and well combined. Stir in the lemon and orange juices and zests and the remaining ½ cup heavy cream and blend well.

Place the ganache-lined pie shell on a rimmed baking sheet. Strain the filling through a fine-mesh sieve directly into the pie shell, or strain it into a separate bowl and then pour it into the shell. Bake on the middle rack of the oven for 25 to 30 minutes, rotating 180 degrees when the edges start to set, 15 to 20 minutes through baking. The pie is finished when the edges are set and the center is no longer liquid but still quite wobbly. Be careful not to overbake or the custard can separate. The filling will continue to cook and set after the pie is removed from the oven. Allow to cool completely on a wire rack, 2 to 3 hours. Serve slightly warm, at room temperature, or cool.

The pie will keep refrigerated for 2 days or at room temperature for 1 day.

Maple Lime Custard Pie

Makes one 9-inch pie
Serves 8 to 10

One wouldn't expect that a salad dressing could inspire a pie recipe. When we found ourselves in a discussion on our ambitions for creating our take on Key lime pie with our talented friend and photographer of this book, Andrea Gentl, she mentioned a delicious maple lime salad dressing she had created for her blog, *Hungry Ghost Food & Travel*. We jumped at the suggestion, agreeing that it is an unexpected combination that balances perfectly whether used for sweet or savory dishes.

Pecan Biscotti Crust for a 9-inch pie (see page 214)

Use Grade B maple syrup for a stronger maple flavor. We source ours from Poorfarm Farm; see our "Sourcing" section for more information. Never, ever use imitation maple syrup.

½ cup sour cream
¼ cup granulated sugar
Finely grated zest of ½ lime
½ teaspoon kosher salt
4 large eggs
1 large egg yolk
⅓ cup fresh lime juice (from about 3 limes)
1 cup maple syrup (preferably Grade B)
¼ cup heavy cream

Position a rack in the center of the oven and preheat the oven to 325°F. Place the prepared crumb shell on a rimmed baking sheet.

Combine the sour cream, granulated sugar, lime zest, and salt in a large bowl and mix well. Beat in the eggs and egg yolk one at a time, mixing well after each addition. Add the lime juice, maple syrup, and heavy cream, and mix until well combined.

Carefully pour the filling into the pie shell; to avoid disturbing the crumb crust, slow the stream by pouring it over a rubber scraper and let the filling dribble into the pan. Bake on the middle rack of the oven for 35 to 40 minutes, rotating 180 degrees when the edges start to set, about 30 minutes through baking. The pie is finished when the edges are set and puffed slightly and the center is no longer liquid but still quite wobbly. Be careful not to overbake or the custard can separate; the filling will continue to cook and set after the pie is removed from the oven. Allow to cool completely on a wire rack, 2 to 3 hours. Serve slightly warm, at room temperature, or cool.

The pie will keep refrigerated for 2 days or at room temperature for 1 day.

Buttermilk Chess Pie

Chess pie is perfect for experimentation—use whatever ingredient you've got on hand and make it the forward note. We like to use some traditional chess pie recipes in the shop, and our simple buttermilk version is a classic and easy-to-make pie that is a definite favorite.

Makes one 9-inch pie
Serves 8 to 10

Cornmeal Crust (or All-Butter Crust) for a 9-inch single-crust pie (see page 211 or 207), partially prebaked (see page 68)

1 cup granulated sugar

¾ teaspoon ground cinnamon

1 tablespoon all-purpose flour

½ teaspoon kosher salt

7 tablespoons unsalted butter, melted and cooled

1 teaspoon vanilla paste (or vanilla extract)

⅔ cup sour cream

3 large eggs

1 large egg yolk

1⅓ cups buttermilk

1 teaspoon white vinegar

About three-quarters of the way through baking, sprinkle the top of the pie with ⅛ teaspoon sugar mixed with ⅛ teaspoon cinnamon for an extra fragrant note.

Position a rack in the center of the oven and preheat the oven to 325°F. Place the prebaked pie shell on a rimmed baking sheet.

In a large bowl whisk together the sugar, cinnamon, flour, and salt. Whisk in the melted butter and vanilla paste. Add the sour cream and whisk until smooth. Add the eggs one at a time, then the egg yolk, then the buttermilk and vinegar, whisking well after each addition.

Strain the filling through a fine-mesh sieve directly into the pie shell, or strain it into a separate bowl and then pour it into the shell. Bake on the middle rack of the oven for 45 to 55 minutes, rotating 180 degrees when the edges start to set, 30 to 35 minutes through baking. The pie is finished when the edges are set and puffed slightly and the center is no longer liquid but still quite wobbly. Be careful not to overbake or the custard can separate; the filling will continue to cook and set after the pie is removed from the oven. Allow to cool completely on a wire rack, 2 to 3 hours. Serve slightly warm, at room temperature, or cool.

The pie will keep refrigerated for 2 days or at room temperature for 1 day.

Green Chili Chocolate Pie

Makes one 9-inch tart
Serves 8 to 10

Rather than using the traditional cayenne powder or red chilis, we chose jalapeño for this pie, which adds an unexpected "green" freshness to the chocolate, with a mild heat for a pie that is rich and bold.

Chocolate All-Butter Crust for a single-crust pie (see page 210), partially prebaked in a 9-inch springform pan (see page 68)

This pie can also be made in a regular tart pan, but the springform is a unique way to create a different shape; experiment with it if you have one in your tool collection.

1 jalapeño pepper, halved and sliced into ½-inch pieces
1-inch piece fresh ginger, peeled and sliced into ⅛-inch pieces
1 cup whole milk
1 cup heavy cream
12 ounces bittersweet chocolate (55% cocoa), broken into ¼-inch pieces
½ teaspoon ground cardamom
½ teaspoon kosher salt
2 large eggs
2 teaspoons fresh lime juice

Position a rack in the center of the oven and preheat the oven to 325°F. Place the prebaked springform pan on a rimmed baking sheet.

Combine the sliced jalapeño (with seeds), sliced ginger, milk, and cream in a heavy-bottomed saucepan and bring just to a boil. Remove from the heat, cover, and allow to steep for 6 to 8 minutes.

Combine the chocolate, cardamom, and salt in a large heatproof bowl and position a fine-mesh sieve over the top. Bring the cream mixture back to a simmer, and immediately strain it over the top of the chocolate. Let stand for 5 minutes, and then whisk steadily until all the chocolate is melted.

Crack the eggs into a separate bowl or large measuring cup, and whisk. Slowly stream a small amount of the chocolate mixture into the eggs, whisking as you pour. Continue until the egg mixture feels warm to the touch; then mix it back into the chocolate mixture. Add the lime juice and whisk until smooth.

Strain the filling through a fine-mesh sieve directly into the springform pan, or strain it into a separate bowl and then pour it into the pan. Bake on the middle rack of the oven for 30 to 35 minutes, rotating 180 degrees when the edges start to set, 20 to 25 minutes through baking. The pie is finished when the edges are set about 2 inches in and puffed slightly and the center is no longer liquid but still quite wobbly. Be careful not to overbake or the filling will be dry and sandy; the filling will continue to cook and set after the pie is removed from the oven. Allow to cool completely on a wire rack, 2 to 3 hours. Serve slightly warm or at room temperature.

The pie will keep refrigerated for 2 days or at room temperature for 1 day.

Crusts

Make it by hand—at least give it a try.

A mutual passion for executing the perfect piecrust was probably what truly started us on our journey into pie making. While Emily had gotten excited about making pies from a sculptural, hands-on perspective, it was Melissa who would take our crust recipe and tweak it (over and over again) to perfection with the addition of cider vinegar for tang and tenderness. To this day you might still find us arguing about perfect crust execution, but we definitely agree that to work in our kitchen, you must have the ability to make a good crust, no matter the size or temperature of your hands. In our opinion, when it comes to baking pie for yourself and your friends and family, it's all about how you, the pie maker, handle it, and not what a machine can do for you.

All-Butter Crust

Our signature and most popular crust, with a hint of cider vinegar for tang and tenderness.

Single-Crust Pie

1¼ cups unbleached all-purpose flour

½ teaspoon kosher salt

1½ teaspoons granulated sugar

¼ pound (1 stick) cold unsalted butter, cut into ½-inch pieces

½ cup cold water

2 tablespoons cider vinegar

½ cup ice

Makes dough for one single-crust 9- to 10-inch pie or tart

Double-Crust Pie

2½ cups unbleached all-purpose flour

1 teaspoon kosher salt

1 tablespoon granulated sugar

½ pound (2 sticks) cold unsalted butter, cut into ½-inch pieces

1 cup cold water

¼ cup cider vinegar

1 cup ice

Makes dough for one double-crust 9- to 10-inch pie or tart

Stir the flour, salt, and sugar together in a large bowl. Add the butter pieces and coat with the flour mixture using a bench scraper or spatula. With a pastry blender, cut the butter into the flour mixture, working quickly until mostly pea-size pieces of butter remain (a few larger pieces are okay; be careful not to overblend).

Combine the water, cider vinegar, and ice in a large measuring cup or small bowl. Sprinkle 2 tablespoons of the ice water mixture over the flour mixture, and mix and cut it in with a bench scraper or spatula until it is fully incorporated. Add more of the ice water mixture, 1 to 2 tablespoons at a time, using the bench scraper or your hands (or both) to mix until the dough comes together in a ball, with some dry bits remaining. Squeeze and pinch with your fingertips to bring all the dough together, sprinkling dry bits with more small drops of the ice water mixture, if necessary, to combine. Shape the dough into a flat disc, wrap in plastic, and refrigerate for at least 1 hour, preferably overnight, to give the crust time to mellow. If making the double-crust version, divide the dough in half before shaping each portion into flat discs.

Wrapped tightly, the dough can be refrigerated for 3 days or frozen for 1 month.

Lard & Butter Crust

If you are a fan of lard crusts, use this recipe in place of any of the recipes that call for our All-Butter Crust. Be sure to use a nice rendered leaf lard—check with a local pork producer or butcher for it; they might even set some aside for you like our friends at the Meat Hook in Brooklyn have done for us.

Makes dough for one single-crust 9- to 10-inch pie or tart

Single-Crust Pie

1¼ cups unbleached all-purpose flour

½ teaspoon kosher salt

1½ teaspoons granulated sugar

4 tablespoons (½ stick) cold unsalted butter, cut into ½-inch pieces

¼ cup very cold or frozen rendered leaf lard, cut into ½-inch pieces

½ cup cold water

2 tablespoons cider vinegar

½ cup ice

Makes dough for one double-crust 9- to 10-inch pie or tart

Double-Crust Pie

2½ cups unbleached all-purpose flour

1 teaspoon kosher salt

1 tablespoon granulated sugar

¼ pound (1 stick) cold unsalted butter, cut into ½-inch pieces

½ cup very cold or frozen rendered leaf lard, cut into ½-inch pieces

1 cup cold water

4 tablespoons cider vinegar

1 cup ice

Stir the flour, salt, and sugar together in a large bowl. Add the butter pieces and lard and coat with the flour mixture using a bench scraper or spatula. With a pastry blender, cut the butter into the flour mixture, working quickly until mostly pea-size pieces of butter remain (a few larger pieces are okay; be careful not to overblend).

Combine the water, cider vinegar, and ice in a large measuring cup or bowl. Sprinkle 2 tablespoons of the ice water mixture over the flour mixture, and mix and cut it in with a bench scraper or spatula until it is fully incorporated. Add more of the ice water mixture, 1 to 2 tablespoons at a time, and mix until the dough comes together in a ball, with some dry bits remaining. Squeeze and pinch with your fingertips to bring all the dough together, sprinkling dry bits with more small drops of the ice water mixture, if necessary, to combine. Shape the dough into a flat disc, wrap in plastic, and refrigerate for at least 1 hour, preferably overnight, to give the crust time to mellow. If making the double-crust version, divide the dough in half before shaping each portion into flat discs.

Wrapped tightly, the dough can be refrigerated for 3 days or frozen for 1 month.

Animal Cracker Crumb Crust

You read that right: animal crackers make an awesome crumb crust.

Makes one 9-inch piecrust

5 ounces animal crackers (about 75 crackers)
2 tablespoons granulated sugar
¼ teaspoon kosher salt
5 tablespoons unsalted butter, melted

In the bowl of a food processor fitted with the blade attachment, grind the crackers to fine crumbs. Add the sugar, salt, and melted butter and pulse just to incorporate.

Pour the crumbs into an ungreased, preferably metal 9-inch pie pan. Spread evenly over the bottom; then create a circle about 1 inch in to separate the crumbs for the sides from the crumbs for the bottom. Start pressing the outer ring of crumbs evenly up the sides and into the corner (where the side meets the bottom) of the pan. Press the remaining crumbs evenly over the bottom to meet the sides; use a flat-bottomed cup to smooth out bumps. Freeze until solid, about 10 minutes. If not prebaking the crust, keep chilled until ready to fill.

If prebaking, preheat the oven to 350°F. Bake on the center oven rack for 15 minutes, until fragrant and darkened slightly. If the crust slumps or cracks while baking, gently push the crumbs back into place, while hot, with a clean, folded kitchen towel. Cool completely on a wire rack. Refrigerate the crust prior to filling to set the crumbs in place to make filling easier.

Chocolate All-Butter Crust

This is essentially our all-butter crust with high-quality cocoa powder blended in. Valrhona makes a beautiful cocoa powder, but any high-quality chocolate maker's powder would be a good choice to achieve a rich chocolate flavor.

Makes dough for one single-crust 9- to 10-inch pie or tart

Single-Crust Pie

1 cup unbleached all-purpose flour

¼ cup cocoa powder

½ teaspoon kosher salt

1½ teaspoons granulated sugar

¼ pound (1 stick) cold unsalted butter, cut into ½-inch pieces

½ cup cold water

2 tablespoons cider vinegar

½ cup ice

Stir the flour, cocoa, salt, and sugar together in a large bowl. Add the butter pieces and coat with the flour mixture using a bench scraper or spatula. With a pastry blender, cut the butter into the flour mixture, working quickly until mostly pea-size pieces of butter remain (a few larger pieces are okay; be careful not to overblend).

Combine the water, cider vinegar, and ice in a large measuring cup or small bowl. Sprinkle 2 tablespoons of the ice water mixture over the flour mixture, and mix and cut it in with a bench scraper or spatula until it is fully incorporated. Add more of the ice water mixture, 1 to 2 tablespoons at a time, and mix until the dough comes together in a ball, with some dry bits remaining. Squeeze and pinch with your fingertips to bring all the dough together, sprinkling dry bits with more small drops of the ice water mixture, if necessary, to combine. Shape the dough into a flat disc, wrap in plastic, and refrigerate for at least 1 hour, preferably overnight, to give the crust time to mellow.

Wrapped tightly, the dough can be refrigerated for 3 days or frozen for 1 month.

Cornmeal Crust

Adding cornmeal to a crust gives it a toothy body that pairs nicely with almost any fruit pie, and a lot of our custards as well.

Single-Crust Pie

1 cup unbleached all-purpose flour

¼ cup stone-ground cornmeal

½ teaspoon kosher salt

1½ teaspoons granulated sugar

¼ pound (1 stick) cold unsalted butter, cut into ½-inch pieces

½ cup cold water

2 tablespoons cider vinegar

½ cup ice

Makes dough for one single-crust 9- to 10-inch pie

Double-Crust Pie

2 cups unbleached all-purpose flour

½ cup stone-ground cornmeal

1 teaspoon kosher salt

3 teaspoons granulated sugar

½ pound (2 sticks) cold unsalted butter, cut into ½-inch pieces

1 cup cold water

4 tablespoons cider vinegar

1 cup ice

Makes dough for one double-crust 9- to 10-inch pie

Stir the flour, cornmeal, salt, and sugar together in a large bowl. Add the butter pieces and coat with the flour mixture using a spatula. With a pastry blender, cut the butter into the flour mixture, working quickly until mostly pea-size pieces of butter remain (a few larger pieces are okay; be careful not to overblend).

Combine the water, cider vinegar, and ice in a large measuring cup or small bowl. Sprinkle 2 tablespoons of the ice water mixture over the flour mixture, and mix and cut it in with a bench scraper or spatula until it is fully incorporated. Add more of the ice water mixture, 1 to 2 tablespoons at a time, and mix until the dough comes together in a ball, with some dry bits remaining. Squeeze and pinch with your fingertips to bring all the dough together, sprinkling dry bits with more small drops of the ice water mixture, if necessary, to combine. Shape the dough into a flat disc, wrap in plastic, and refrigerate for at least 1 hour, preferably overnight, to give the crust time to mellow. If making the double-crust version, divide the dough in half before shaping each portion into flat discs.

Wrapped tightly, the dough can be refrigerated for 3 days or frozen for 1 month.

Gingersnap Crumb Crust

This was the first crumb crust to be served in the pie shop, and it's pretty addictive if you like gingersnaps. We make a fresh gingersnap cookie and then blend it into a crust. Store-bought gingersnaps work equally well.

Makes one 9-inch piecrust

About twenty 2-inch gingersnap cookies (enough to make 1 cup crumbs)
2 tablespoons granulated sugar
¼ teaspoon kosher salt
4 tablespoons (½ stick) unsalted butter, melted
Egg white wash (1 large egg white whisked with 1 teaspoon cold water) [optional]

In the bowl of a food processor fitted with the blade attachment, grind the gingersnap cookies to fine crumbs. Add the sugar, salt, and melted butter and pulse just to incorporate.

Pour the crumbs into an ungreased, preferably metal 9-inch pie pan. Spread evenly over the bottom, and then create a circle about 1 inch in to separate the crumbs for the sides from the crumbs for the bottom. Start pressing the outer ring of crumbs evenly up the sides and into the corner (where the side meets the bottom) of the pan. Press the remaining crumbs evenly over the bottom to meet the sides; use a flat-bottomed cup to smooth out bumps. Freeze until solid, about 10 minutes. Preheat the oven to 350°F.

Bake on the center oven rack for 12 to 14 minutes, until fragrant and darkened slightly. If the crust slumps or cracks while baking, gently push the crumbs back into place, while hot, with a clean, folded kitchen towel. While hot from the oven, moistureproof the crust by brushing the bottom lightly with the egg white wash, if desired. Bake for an additional minute to set the egg white wash. Cool completely on a wire rack. Refrigerate the crust for 10 minutes prior to filling to set the crumbs in place to make filling easier.

Pistachio Coconut Crust

Gluten-free, no-bake, and awesome.

½ cup plus 1 tablespoon shelled pistachios, raw and unsalted
½ cup plus 1 tablespoon unsweetened shredded coconut
3 tablespoons granulated sugar
¼ teaspoon kosher salt

Makes one 9-inch
piecrust

In a dry medium-size skillet, toast the pistachios over medium heat until fragrant, 7 to 9 minutes; shake the pan or stir frequently to prevent burning. Pour into a shallow dish and allow to cool, about 10 minutes. Meanwhile, toast the coconut in the same skillet over medium-low heat, 2 to 3 minutes or until lightly golden and fragrant. When finished, immediately add to the pistachios.

Once cool, pour the toasted pistachios and coconut plus the sugar and salt into the bowl of a food processor fitted with the blade attachment. Process until the pistachios are finely chopped and the mixture looks homogenous, scraping down if necessary; the crumbs will stick together slightly when ready.

Pour the crumbs into an ungreased, preferably metal 9-inch pie pan. Spread evenly over the bottom; then create a circle about 1 inch in to separate the crumbs for the sides from the crumbs for the bottom. Start pressing the outer ring of crumbs evenly up the sides and into the corner (where the side meets the bottom) of the pan. Press the remaining crumbs evenly over the bottom to meet the sides; use a flat-bottomed cup to smooth out bumps. Freeze until solid, at least 10 minutes, before filling.

Pecan Biscotti Crust

In the shop, we make our own pecan biscotti and then grind them to make this crust. Ladyfingers are a perfectly good, easily available substitute.

Makes one 9-inch piecrust

2½ ounces ladyfingers (about 8 cookies)
2 tablespoons granulated sugar
¼ teaspoon kosher salt
½ cup pecan pieces
3 tablespoons unsalted butter, melted

Place the ladyfingers in a zippered plastic storage bag and crush with a rolling pin until they are medium-fine pieces.

In the bowl of a food processor fitted with the blade attachment, grind the ladyfinger pieces, along with the sugar and salt, until they are fine crumbs. Add the pecan pieces and process until the mixture is homogenous. Add the melted butter and process just until combined.

Pour the crumbs into an ungreased, preferably metal 9-inch pie pan. Spread evenly over the bottom; then create a circle about 1 inch in to separate the crumbs for the sides from the crumbs for the bottom. Start pressing the outer ring of crumbs evenly up the sides and into the corner (where the side meets the bottom) of the pan. Press the remaining crumbs evenly over the bottom to meet the sides; use a flat-bottomed measuring cup to smooth out bumps. Freeze until solid, about 10 minutes. Meanwhile, position a rack in the center of the oven and preheat the oven to 375°F.

Place the crust on a rimmed baking sheet and bake on the center oven rack for about 14 minutes, until lightly browned. If the crust slumps or cracks while baking, gently push the crumbs back into place, while hot, with a clean, folded kitchen towel. Cool completely on a wire rack. Refrigerate the crust for 10 minutes prior to filling to set the crumbs in place to make filling easier.

Saltine Crust

This is a unique crust that is also pretty easy. We recommend using crackers with unsalted tops to prevent the crust from being, well, just too salty.

About 30 unsalted tops saltine crackers (enough for 1 cup crumbs)
3 tablespoons granulated sugar
5 tablespoons unsalted butter, melted

Makes one 9-inch
piecrust

In the bowl of a food processor fitted with the blade attachment, grind the crackers to fine crumbs. Add the sugar and melted butter and pulse just to incorporate.

Pour the crumbs into an ungreased 9-inch pie pan. Spread evenly over the bottom; then create a circle about 1 inch in to separate the crumbs for the sides from the crumbs for the bottom. Start pressing the outer ring of crumbs evenly up the sides and into the corner (where the side meets the bottom) of the pan. Press the remaining crumbs evenly over the bottom to meet the sides; use a flat-bottomed cup to smooth out bumps. Freeze until solid, about 10 minutes. If not prebaking the crust, keep chilled until ready to fill. If prebaking, preheat the oven to 350°F.

Bake on the center oven rack for 14 to 16 minutes, until fragrant and darkened slightly. If the crust slumps or cracks while baking, gently push the crumbs back into place, while hot, with a clean, folded kitchen towel. Cool completely on a wire rack. Refrigerate the crust for 10 minutes prior to filling to set the crumbs in place to make filling easier.

Oat Crumble Topping & Crust

The recipe can be used as a crumble topping or a crust. For crust, just press it in the pan bottom for a delicious, crunchy oat crust.

Makes 2 cups, enough for one 9-inch pie topping or crust

2 tablespoons granulated sugar
¼ cup packed light brown sugar
¾ cup rolled oats
⅓ cup all-purpose flour
½ teaspoon kosher salt
⅛ teaspoon ground allspice
⅛ teaspoon ground cardamom
⅛ teaspoon ground cinnamon
4 tablespoons (½ stick) unsalted butter, cut into ½-inch cubes, at room temperature

Stir together all the ingredients except the butter in a large bowl. Sprinkle in the butter pieces and toss to coat. Rub the butter into the dry ingredients with your fingertips until the butter is incorporated and the mixture is chunky but not homogenous.

If using for a crumble top, chill for at least 15 minutes before using.

If using as a crust, press evenly into the bottom and up the sides of an ungreased, preferably metal 9-inch pie pan. Freeze until solid, about 15 minutes. Meanwhile, preheat the oven to 350°F. Bake on the middle oven rack for 18 to 20 minutes. If the crust slumps or cracks while baking, gently push the crumble back into place, while hot, with a clean, folded kitchen towel. Cool completely before filling.

The crust will keep refrigerated for 5 days or frozen for 1 month.

Streusel Topping

A simple, tasty pie topping.

1 cup all-purpose flour
3 tablespoons packed light brown sugar
4 teaspoons granulated sugar
¼ teaspoon kosher salt
6 tablespoons unsalted butter, cut into ½-inch cubes, at room temperature

Makes 1⅔ cups streusel, enough for one 9- or 10-inch pie topping

Stir together the flour, brown and granulated sugars, and salt in a large bowl. Sprinkle in the butter pieces and toss to coat. Rub the butter into the dry ingredients with your fingertips until the butter is incorporated and the mixture is chunky but not homogenous.

Chill for at least 15 minutes before using.

The streusel will keep refrigerated for 5 days or frozen for 1 month.

Acknowledgments

We would like to give the following thanks:

To our parents, Mary and Ron, for their love, guidance, and support in all that we endeavor. To our brother, Christopher, for his wisdom and intuition. To our extended family, the Zastrows and the Elsens: all of our aunts, uncles, and cousins, each of whom we love and respect.

To Jodie Gatlin for your loving friendship, your immense contribution and work on this book, and your ability to make everything look good with style. We couldn't have done this without you.

To Andrea Gentl and Marty Hyers for your friendship, inspiring imagery, and for making our pies look delectable. To Anna Shillinglaw-Hampton, Meredith Munn, Alpha Smoot, and Sara Glick for your wonderful work and support on the shoots.

To Jenni Ferrari Adler for being a fantastic, supportive agent, encouraging us every step of the way and always at the right moments. To Sally Wofford-Girand and the team at Union Literary for enthusiastically supporting our book.

To the great team of Grand Central Life & Style for your enthusiasm, insight, and guidance: Jamie Raab, our editor Karen Murgolo, Pippa White, Elizabeth Connor, Thomas Whatley, Kallie Shimek, Anne Twomey, and Sonya Safro.

To Laura Palese for your fantastic help with this book.

To Kendra McKnight, Justine Delaney, Sara Franklin, and Kate Hays for your on-point help and insight with recipe testing, your friendship and continued support.

To Inez Valk-Kempthorne and Justus Kempthorne for your true friendship, creative vision, and immense contribution in helping Four & Twenty Blackbirds move out of a home kitchen into a real business, and for your continued support.

To Stephanie Dedes-Reimers and Inez Valk-Kempthorne for designing and painting the beautiful hand-painted rug in the pie shop.

A giant heartfelt thank-you to the entire staff of Four & Twenty Blackbirds, past and present; we would be nothing without your hard work and dedication to the shop; you are family to us: Rica Borich, Colleen Riley, Dustin Walker, Thomasin Alter, Toby Bannister, Sara Franklin, Ali Rudel, Casey Angelo, Megan Fehrenkamp, Marcin Cybula, Kyoko Masutani, Meghan Haas, Christa Corle, Danielle Dillon, Lisa Kolarsick, Jessica Denzer, Stephanie Valada-Viars, Stephen Reader, Nathaniel Taylor-Leach, Alice Pencavel, Juan Pablo Baene, Sam White, Nicole Evangelista, Ryan Taylor, Liam Martin, Janel Sellers, Nick

Carbone, Jon Leland, Janessa Goodman, Alice Maggio, Zoe Kanan, Rick Visser, Marisa Wu, Justine Delaney, Eli Winograd, Kristine Valmonte, Irene Davidson, Elizabeth Mueller, Kamel Fedoul, Kate Blemler, Kathleen Crosby, Lisa Ludwinski, Evan Dorfman, Anna-Shillinglaw Hampton, Sean Twigg, Brian Feeney, Olivia Lerner, Danielle Swift, Julia Ehrman, Merisa Skinner, Hillary Fann, Alyssa Barone, Bobby Blackman, Liz Parlin, Vicki Copeland, Jena Derman, Jill Peters, Amber Kempthorne, Jonathan Lear, Merida Gorman, Katelyn Smith, Julian Rich, Tippi Clark, Chris Robinson, Megan Stockton, Kylie Gilchrist, Grant Tucker, Zak McLongstreet. And to those we may have missed, thank you for your contribution.

We are grateful to our friends, neighbors, and colleagues for your enduring support and help over the years: Audrey Harris, April Frick, Rachel Ostrow, Kayla Stearns, Benjamin Cohen, chef Chris Bradley, Mike Rodriguez, Frieda and Kevin and Blaize, Oona, Flynt, Francelle, and Michael, Geraldine Levine (for being a thoughtful, encouraging voice and far more than just our landlord) and Felix, Jill Mercedes, Trisha Mulligan, Terence Taylor, Keion Charles, Angela Conant, Xylia Buros, Robin Raisfeld and Rob Patronite, Scott Bridi, Rachel Wharton, Marc Sklar, Gabriel Rivera and his fig trees, Eve Sussman, Simon Lee, Lee Boronson, Evan Strusinski, Sam Richman, Amy Thielen, the 8th Street Block Association, Julius Lang and Joe O'Dea, Todd Selby, Michael Pantone, the Svensens: Betty, Bill, and Matt, Hubert Burzynski, Alan Young, the family of Wilklow Orchards especially Albert, Fred, and Becky, Nate Smith and Sophie Kamin, Steve Hindy and Ellen Foote, Danny Meyer, Richard Corraine, Marisa Wu and Salty Road, Frank Falcinelli and Frank Castronovo, Alexandra Penfold, Rob and Lisa Howard, Julian Richards, Miranda Lloyd, Eugene Jho, Atom Cianfarani, Maya Suess, Jeanette and Mike Abbink, Adam Reimers, Abe Kempthorne, Stephan von Muehlen, Chris Cole, Lauren Lintvent, Julian Brizzi and Rucola, Michael Hu and Hana Kitchens, Irving Farm Coffee Roasters, Table on Ten, Lark Café. Our Gowanus neighbors: The Gowanus Studio Space, Brooklyn Homebrew, Tin House, Joel Bukiewicz and Cut Brooklyn, Carver and Sonya Farrell and The Pines, The Pilates Garage, Michael & Ping's, Fletcher's Brooklyn Barbecue, Crop to Cup Coffee Roasters, Ben Toht and The Saline Project, Ruth Lingen and the staff of Pace Prints.

Thank you to all of our customers and community for your support and appetite for pie. It is our pleasure to bake for you; we love you!

We apologize to anyone we may have left out, but thank you.

With love,
Em and Mel

Index

About the Authors

Sisters **Emily Elsen** and **Melissa Elsen** were born and raised in the rural farm town of Hecla, South Dakota. Their mother and her sisters owned and operated the popular local restaurant, the Calico Kitchen, for which their grandmother Liz made all the pies. After pursuing different careers—Melissa in finance and Emily in sculpture and photography—they established their business in Brooklyn. They originally custom-baked pies in their apartment before opening Four & Twenty Blackbirds pie and coffee shop in 2010. Named "Artisan of the Year" by *Time Out New York* in 2011, they have received critical praise for their pies and have been featured in a variety of food media including the Food Network and the Cooking Channel, in the *New York Times, Martha Stewart Living,* and *New York* magazine.